CW00821568

NEVER TAKE NO FOR
AN ANSWER

Best wishes

Marilyn

NEVER TAKE NO FOR AN ANSWER

Marilyn Hawes

The Book Guild Ltd
Sussex, England

First published in Great Britain in 2004 by
The Book Guild Ltd
25 High Street
Lewes, East Sussex
BN7 2LU

Copyright © Marilyn Hawes 2004

The right of Marilyn Hawes to be identified as the author of
this work has been asserted by her in accordance with the
Copyright, Designs and Patents Act 1988.

All rights reserved. No part of this publication may be
reproduced, transmitted, or stored in a retrieval system, in any
form or by any means, without permission in writing from the
publisher, nor be otherwise circulated in any form of binding or
cover other than that in which it is published and without a
similar condition being imposed on the subsequent purchaser.

Typesetting in Times by
Keyboard Services, Luton, Bedfordshire

Printed in Great Britain by
CPI Bath

A catalogue record for this book is available from
The British Library

ISBN 1 85776 883 3

Contents

Preface

I never realised my life experiences were preparation for the emotional trauma I would face in 2002. The opportunity to write this book has been the only way to release and express those emotions. My healing process began here. I hope my story will help others.

On Sunday evening, 7th December 1952, the midwife was on her way to evensong when my parents called her to say my birth was imminent. One look at me convinced my father of Charles Darwin's theory that humans had evolved from apes.

Not many hours old, it was discovered I was suffering from a gastric illness which could have killed me. My mother's grit and determination to feed me regardless of the terrible problems she experienced with breast feeding, saved my life. Marilyn was not going to 'roll over and die' – and it has been that way ever since!

On reflection, I think my parents would have the right to say I was a difficult and different child with a strong will, always questioning, always challenging. My father taught me by example never to accept the unacceptable, and also to see the 'bigger picture'. My mother taught me by her own example to have the mental strength to keep going through all adversity. Armed with that cocktail I learnt quickly to achieve what I wanted and how I wanted to achieve it, even though it didn't suit others' plans for me!

I challenged the nuns at school – rules and aspects of Catholicism, which to my thinking didn't make sense. I refused to go to university because the nuns said I should!

In 1976, I married David and was living in Basingstoke. It was my dad's birthday – 3rd February 1977. I was 23. My friend, the wife of my colleague, rang me at work telling me she had killed her children, which is another story for another time.

In 1978, David and I moved to Wokingham, Berkshire. I found a career in teaching – I was told it was impossible without a degree but went on to teach music to the children of some very famous people.

I fought successfully to have four children; having had four miscarriages, doctors said I might not be able to sustain pregnancies. In 1980 I had Christopher, in 1982 I had Nicky and in 1986 I gave birth to twin boys, Peter and Michael. Tales of their under-five activities is definitely another book.

My father died in August 1994, a shock to us all, only to be followed in August 1995 by the drowning of my friend's son in a boating accident on holiday in France. At such a dreadful time, I had to help my friend and family. And in August 2001 my boss and friend died of cancer minutes after I arrived to visit, and on her daughter's 21st birthday – what to say? How to comfort? What to do? To this day, I dislike the month of August.

I had left what had become an unworkable marriage. Divorcing in 1996, unable to sell the house, I finally shut the door on the family home in March 1997, making four children homeless. Naturally, we survived – I had to make it happen and went on months later to buy my own house.

My friends advised against me marrying a man I had met through an introduction agency, but I ignored them and married Roger Norman Woods on 29th April 2000, and we moved to Billingshurst, West Sussex.

Life here has been challenging. We survive because both Roger and I have learnt to 'grow a spine' in order to cope with the knock-backs we had when we were younger. Just as important is faith, belief in your mission and the courage to see it through. Someone once told me that courage is hope wrapped in prayer.

Anyway, all this is another book. So how did I get to be at the Court of Appeal, never having been in a court in my life?

1

The Joys of Motherhood?!

David and I had met in church in 1964, in Southampton, when I was 12 and he was 18. Church attendance was a way of life and so it was natural that we would raise our children in the same way.

Christopher was the easiest of children until this one day in St Sebastian's Church family service. He was born several months after my first miscarriage.

Doctors tried to advise me that I had one lovely little boy and to be thankful for what I had. I was thankful, very thankful, but I thought, 'I have managed to produce one healthy child after a miscarriage so who's to say I can't do it again and again!' So I persevered!

What is it in a two-year-old's mind that in a heartbeat makes them flick a switch from the normally gorgeous to the irascibly monstrous?

It was the summer of 1982, we were running late this particular morning and in a rush to get to the church on time. I gathered up all sorts of goodies and distractions to keep our Christopher quiet through what can only be described as a yawning bore for a young child. I was already six months pregnant with my second child Nicola. She followed two miscarriages after having Christopher.

I believe the congregation were singing a hymn about peace and stillness as they progressed up the aisle for Communion. The candles were glowing and there was a tangible sense of expectation and spirit in the air.

Suddenly and uncharacteristically, Christopher started wailing. 'Me no want Todas tank engine – me wanted Poteman Pat van' – translated, of course, as 'Thomas the Tank Engine' and 'Postman Pat van'. Poor Thomas came crashing down with a resounding crack onto the wooden pew! And more: 'My bikit is broke', or 'my biscuit has broken'. And then: 'Me like bibena not obange' – you got it, 'Ribena not orange'. I won't even bother mentioning his opinion of the selection of little books and cuddlies I had stuffed in my enormous holdall!

It was then our turn to leave the sanctuary of our pew for all to see! What is the fascination with car keys and children? Willing to try anything to shut him up, I let him carry them up the aisle. All was going well until he suddenly decided to wing a missile at the vicar! Only just smiling, while at the same time wanting to wring his tiny neck, I returned to the pew, relieved no longer to be on public view and convinced that next time he would definitely be in the crèche! I could not believe the demon that had come over him.

At the end of the service this very pleasant silver-haired man, with the most gorgeous brown eyes, leant forward from the pew behind and said, 'I really admire you and the way you handled your little boy – what a great mum. Oh, by the way, I am Jeff Carney the new headmaster at the church primary school here.'

At that moment I had had my first meeting with the man who was to become our close family friend and my closest, most respected, trusted and best platonic male friend ever; the man who would eventually break my heart, changing my life forever...

I was 29 when I met him and I am now 51. How was I to know he had already molested a young boy on several occasions?

His Christian way of living and involvement with the Anglican Church was clear for all to see. No one doubted his integrity. If they did, I certainly never heard it and to my knowledge nobody else did either.

So we all introduced ourselves and had coffee with him after the service, and those meetings and chats after church continued. We thought how gentle he was and yet strong – a great combination. He would chat on about the changes he wanted to make in the school and how he was challenging the diocese for money to upgrade the decor and so on. He was charming with a warm disposition, totally committed to achieving his goals.

Both David and I were impressed with his vision for the school and its development. He definitely had a real understanding and empathy for children and all their little quirks and anxieties, even though he was not a father himself. He clearly knew about the best environment in which to educate children and had created a loving and Christian ethos for the school, which we, as parents, could relate to and therefore would be seeking for our own children in the future.

Over coffee on Sundays, he explained his past. Born a Yorkshireman, he had, when younger, been a scout leader and had been in the army during conscription. Some of the stories he would tell about the army life were hilarious – he had a great sense of humour and an understated charisma. He described his dad as a 'bit of a gypsy', always travelling round and Jeff had obviously led a varied life.

He had got into teaching during his time as a non-teaching assistant in Reading, where a teacher he was working with recognised his ability to work with children and suggested he should train professionally to be a teacher.

At about the age of 40 he came out of teaching, having decided to test his faith within a monastery, and began training to become a Franciscan monk. However, he decided after ten months it wasn't really for him and returned to the teaching arena, where his heart really lay.

At one point, Jeff asked us where we would be sending Christopher to school – another joy of becoming a parent! Chris was only two, so it seemed irrelevant. However, Jeff explained that in the local area if one chose a small church primary school, of which there were only two, it was a little like Eton and names had to be put on the list as soon as possible. David and I were amazed that we had apparently to make this decision when Chris was so young. So off we went to explore all the potential local schools.

I had always wanted the children to attend a church school, as I had done, but we looked at four or five schools in total. All we gained was a feeling of total confusion.

One Sunday after church, we spoke to Jeff and explained our dilemma. He told us that as we had a little boy it would be better for him to have a male teacher on the staff for discipline, football, rugby, etc. It seemed to make sense, and there was little difference between Finchampstead Church Primary School and St Sebastian's Church Primary, other than the fact that the latter had a headmaster who was on a mission to develop a school to get on the map.

Shortly after Nicola was born in November 1982, we visited Jeff and took Christopher around to see the school. We were both impressed with the gentle yet firm way he spoke and dealt with Chris, and how he was showing Chris the gerbils and the school budgie, named Bassie, which had been discovered flying freely in the woods. The pupils adopted him and took him home at weekends on a rota basis.

So that was it – we put Chris's name down to start in 1985, which seemed an age away. Happy to be over that parental hurdle we carried on with our life and continued to lose and produce babies.

2

Brain Decay

Nicola had the complete opposite nature to Chris. She bounced into the world like a champagne cork, screaming her head off. The nurses said, 'Oh, the baby is hours away yet', and within the next ten minutes there she was!

Why was I surprised to find her a challenging child over the next 20 years? She was her mother's daughter. My own mum was delighted to see that at last I was experiencing some of the hell I had given her!

Nicky screamed with colic for the first four months. She ranted and raved for the next three years. She would stamp her feet and stomp off into another room with her nappied bottom sticking out behind like a duck's arse. As soon as she could walk, aged eleven months, she would throw herself down the stairs in a purple rage. I took her to the doctor, as I thought she was having fits. He laughed and said, 'Marilyn, were you a difficult child? Didn't you know this behaviour is genetic?'

'Oh, joy,' I thought. 'One day, you have it all to come to you, young lady!' I hoped that by then I would be living miles away from her!

I should have known Nicky would inherit my love of music – she could hit top C effortlessly from the

7

day she was born. Poor Chris was not impressed. His sister wasn't quite the playmate I had promised him. I was once taking care of a neighbour's baby when Chris had the screaming abdabs, declaring that he didn't want another baby because Nicky wasn't very nice. He thought I had magically produced a brother for him.

Nicky was difficult and determined at every level of life. She refused to be cuddled to sleep. She was 14 months before she sought to be cuddled, saying 'tuddle me, mummy'. I was overjoyed to think maybe she was normal after all!

Chris was three and a half when he needed a minor operation. David was looking after Nicky that day and she decided *this* was the moment when she would become potty-trained – in the park!! Some months later, it was the Christmas playgroup photo for Chris, and it was suggested how lovely it would be to have a photo of little sister alongside him. She was determined not to smile, as I had had the temerity to put her in a dress when she preferred to wear trousers like her brother.

As time went on Nicky wore me down. She was a constant challenge and I began to wonder where my brain had gone! I have always needed mental stimulation and whilst Nicky was a challenge in one sense, I was beginning to feel brain-dead in another.

Chris started school as a 'rising five' in the spring term of 1985. I was sad to see him start school at four years eight months old. He still seemed so little and vulnerable, but this of course left me alone with the troublesome Nicky. Regularly, Nicky would creep into the reception class and sit on the mat next to Chris for registration. She never seemed to absorb the idea that she was too young for school – so, kicking and screaming, mother and daughter would leave the school classroom, mother red-faced with embarrassment. Although I loved her to bits, I was desperate to use my brain.

After school one day, having collected Chris I went to see Jeff to discuss whether he thought I would be of any use as a governor. At the time, the school had a vacancy for a diocesan governor, and being a churchgoer, I appeared to qualify. The head of infants at the time, Mrs Lewis felt convinced I had enough to do without taking on more. But Jeff was pleased and thought it a very good idea, so a governor I became. I often would joke with Jeff how Nicky was 'doing my head in', and I wasn't exactly an earth mother even though I loved children.

At first, I couldn't have been more bored being a governor; the endless and seemingly mindless chatting, going round the houses achieving nothing, or so it seemed. I have never been a very good committee person and have always avoided such things like the plague. Meanwhile David had become a member of the parent–teacher association and eventually became the treasurer.

During this time, Jeff and I got to know each other even better. Being a governor and taking the job seriously and responsibly, I went on courses and grasped the idea very quickly that the head teachers needed support these days, the governor's role having taken on a whole new dimension from that of previous years. I would regularly pop in and see Jeff and ask if there were any problems needing the attention of the governors. After school, Jeff would sometimes pop round to see me to chat about school business.

The workload was quite heavy, so the 16 of us governors split into subcommittees. I was on the curriculum committee and the admissions committee. Being a Church-aided school, we had qualifying rules of entry: Church attenders, current siblings already at the school, those living within the parish boundary, right down to the date when the child's name was registered in the first place. We were only able to have an intake of 17 per year, as the school could only manage approximately 110 children from 5 to 11 years old.

I began to really enjoy the work. I was responsible with a couple of others for writing and selecting video material for the sex-education programme, which had become compulsory for schools to have. Jeff would naturally attend some of these meetings to check on progress and suitability. For a while, I also sat in on the delivery of these sessions to the children. Jeff mainly took the classes for the boys, with the deputy head, Mrs Ashfield, taking the girls.

I also found the admissions committee extremely interesting. Gaining a place at the school had become very competitive, with parents anxiously awaiting their acceptance letter, and for our part we did everything accurately and to the letter so as to avoid a parental appeal.

Jeff was by now attaining a superb reputation for himself as a strong and caring head – good with children and staff, and approachable for parents. He had an 'open door' policy which made him popular with all. The school pupils were doing very well academically, and we had a long waiting list for places.

We had become known as the school that was 'good with vulnerable children who had varying needs'. I remember at one point, while still an admissions governor, doing a rough calculation to gauge the number of children with problems we were accepting as a percentage of the total school population. I was always mindful of the children who had no problems to speak of, whose progress might be impaired if we were too heavy with children who had difficulties. Jeff was adamant we should be seen to be taking a Christian attitude to children who perhaps had become unacceptable at other schools because of their behaviour in class. He was talented in dealing with children who had difficulties – particularly boys. At the time I agreed with Jeff that boys appeared to struggle with the educational system sometimes – and I still feel that way.

He would encourage parents to pop in for a chat if they had any concerns. Sometimes this would drive the staff nuts because they were often unable to grab even five minutes of his time.

During this time, encouraged by Jeff, I would often speak as a governor at parent meetings, and so the friendship grew. Jeff would now pop round after school more frequently, maybe having a bite to eat before a governors' meeting. Living in Reading as he did, which was about eight miles away, he would often eat with a few parents or staff, so that he needn't go home only to have to return to Wokingham later. Women, being the way they are, were happy to cook him a meal, particularly as he was not married. I think we all felt we were offering him family warmth.

One day Jeff asked if David would mind if he borrowed me to attend a gathering in Bracknell to do with the church. I assured him David wouldn't mind – so off we went. I was introduced to a long-time close friend and neighbour of Jeff's. He began to tell me about his new relationship, and we continued to chat about it quite openly.

Nicola would then have been approaching three years old, when, after suffering another miscarriage, I discovered I was pregnant again. I was shocked to a state of total disbelief and numbness when on 11th November 1985 the doctors announced I was carrying twins. Because I had difficulty keeping a pregnancy they had decided to give me hormone injections – the 'glue' to make the baby stay in the womb. I had experienced horrendous, brain-splitting headaches, so I was taken off the medication. Once they discovered I was going to have twins, all those problems made sense to the doctors.

Having survived the critical time of the early weeks at 14 weeks gestation David and I considered it safe to take Chris and Nicky to see what we thought was on the scan. The doctor scanned my tummy and announced, 'Oh, look, can you see what I see?' I was instantly very anxious.

Bearing in mind my first-ever pregnancy and miscarriage ended at the time of a scan with the phrase – 'Is this your first baby Mrs Hawes?' 'Yes.' 'Well, I'm afraid the baby's died!' – I couldn't face going through the angst of that again with the children present. I had already made up my mind that there had to be something wrong with the baby. My thoughts were racing when the doctor said, 'Look, Mrs Hawes, can you see the other head?'

My blurted and very audible reply was, 'Oh, my God, it's got two heads.'

'No silly, you are having twins. Look, there they are side by side, sucking their thumbs,' said the doctor, laughing away at her discovery.

Chris and Nicky were ecstatic. 'Oh, clever Mummy, a baby for each of us!' David was also like a cat with two tails. Me, I was mortified – how would I potty-train *two* toddlers? But as the doctor pointed out, 'Mrs Hawes, they haven't been born yet!'

I was in such a state of shock, the news simply

wouldn't sink in – after all, I had always been told I would have difficulty becoming a mum. I was kept at the hospital in shock for a couple of hours while David was dispatched with the children to break the news to my mum.

I calculated that I would have four children all under five-and-a-half years old. How would I get them all in the car? Would I ever get out of the house? How would I go shopping or to the dentist or doctor. How would I bottle feed two babies (breastfeeding was out of the question, especially as I had never been very good at it)? And so I imagined problem after problem.

I returned to Nicky's ballet class later that day and told those assembled mums who were also friends. They all tried to make positive comments whilst stifling a gut-ripping laugh. I went and told Jeff, whose response was similar to that of the ballet friends. The jokes at my expense were endless!

I wasn't sure how I could continue being a governor – what was going to happen to my brain again?

Finally, on 8th April 1986, Peter and Michael were induced and born five minutes apart. Michael was a very weak baby and nearly died. He had a problem with his heart. Nicky had wanted her baby to be a sister, so I broke the news to her by phone by telling her that Michael needed a very special big sister to care for him and watch over him. So that is how it became – Peter was the first-born twin and was Chris's baby, and Michael was Nicky's special charge.

Life was chaos. Friends came every day to help with taking Chris to school and Nicky to playgroup and doing the shopping. Friends would come and help feed the boys and bath them in the evening. They were terrible at night and I was exhausted. We would put a notice on the front door and take the phone off the

13

hook whilst bottle-making. David and I made up 20 bottles every evening. I don't remember the boys ever having warmed milk or ever being winded properly!

When I had to go out friends would babysit in pairs, reluctant to be left alone with four children under six. I found it amusing that for most of the time I was on my own with the children – I didn't come in pairs!

After a few weeks, I became visible in the playground again and life took on a regimentation only known in the armed forces! I would get up at six in the morning and up until the school run everything operated in fifteen-minute time slots until we were in the car. All those shoes, socks, coats, hats, gloves and school bags, and endless letters of request from school for toilet rolls and egg boxes or cornflake packets for arts and crafts. I had lists everywhere, even on the fridge, so that I could remember which baby I had fed and when. My brain was in a complete fog.

When Christopher was seven and on Nicky's fifth birthday, Michael became seriously ill with a stomach bug which nearly killed him. Eileen, my friend, came to look after him while we went off to handle Nicky's trampoline party. On our return, Eileen said how ill she thought Michael had become. We called the doctor and Michael was rushed into hospital straight away. I can still see Peter's face at the doorway – he was so confused, as we rushed off to hospital with Michael wrapped in a blanket. They were 18 months old.

Both Michael and I were in isolation for nine days. He had lost most of his potassium and had caught a bug only usually transmitted in Nigeria. Heaven knows where or how he caught it!

One day, I looked up and there was Jeff peering through the window. He had come to visit us. We chatted on and he gave me his phone number to call if I felt like a break from the hospital, so I phoned the following day. I was covered in all sorts of grot from Michael's insides and I needed a lovely bubble bath, which one of Jeff's lodgers provided. Jeff cooked supper and got a mate to wash my clothes before I returned to the hospital.

This man must be a 'walking saint', so I thought. What an act of Christian friendship. All my friends were impressed, just as we were with his offer of help. This happened a couple of times more, before I finally went home with Michael.

Regularly, Jeff would smile and wave me into his office for a laugh and a chat. He could see I was worn out and exasperated, and sometimes the laughter ended in tears of exasperation. Our friendship, after Michael being so near death, was now established. It was a very easy friendship of varied conversations and jokes – largely within the school arena. Although I loved the children with all my heart, I found life so hard. However, after missing a couple of governors meetings I was back in circulation once more.

The brain was working again, and miraculously still functioning. I could still remember who I was and where I lived – amazing. There was life after twins. Our family attracted lots of attention wherever we went. Looking back, it seems a very special and privileged time, although it didn't feel that way then. The strain of constantly moving, and having very little sleep, was beginning to show. I didn't realise one could be that tired and still stand!

3

The Crossroads

Life continued to be chaotic, the job as governor became ever busier and I was known among the governors as a kind of troubleshooter, unafraid of a challenge or of speaking up for what I believed was right or wrong for the school. I always enjoyed the debate with whomever it concerned. When I was at school, I was chairperson for the debating society – I am not by nature argumentative, nor do I pick a fight, but I have always stood for justice, especially for anyone in a vulnerable situation. My dad always said, 'Oh dear, Marilyn, you can't save the world!'

I would reply, 'No, but I can at least try to make a difference – if no one ever tried, nothing would ever change, Dad!'

He and I would often have lively debates, which drove my mum mad. I missed him so much when he died and still do. Strangely, I feel him closer to me since his death than when he was alive. I know he sits on my shoulder at times whispering in my ear – I can feel his presence.

I had made many friends in Wokingham from having a host of children, including two very close friends – Eileen and Jill – who became godmothers to the twins. Jill went on to become Jeff's school secretary, having spent several months going into school on a voluntary basis to help the children. Jill and Eileen virtually lived at my house while the children were so small – I could never have coped without their help and that of others. Within my circle of friends, I and another friend, Jane, were the only mums to have gone beyond two children. At times I felt I had turned my clock back to the beginning. Most friends now had their children at nursery or school and had more time for themselves.

Eileen had a daughter the same age as Christopher, called Rebecca. She desperately wanted to learn to play the piano. Eileen asked if I would teach Rebecca. 'Don't be daft!' I said. 'I haven't played the ivories myself for about 15 years!'

Anyway, Rebecca being of a similar character to me and my Nicky, refused to take No for an answer, and kept on badgering her Mum and always asked me why I would not teach her. In my heart I thought, 'Help, I can't do this!'

I quickly corrected myself, as those two words are not of frequent use in my vocabulary. I decided there and then – nothing ventured, nothing gained – go for it. I was at the crossroads of a new career, although I didn't see it at the time.

I set about researching music books and gave myself a couple of months to practise and to brush up on rusty areas and set a date to start with Rebecca.

Rebecca proved to be a good pupil, and I discovered I enjoyed teaching, so after a few months I pursued extending my teaching to become a little private business and advertised at the local shop.

Having four small children, the money was useful, and it was another challenge for me to meet. Very quickly, I was teaching up to 21 pupils! The only snag was that all the lessons were after school, as I was teaching seven- and eight-year-olds. So life at teatime was horrendous.

The twins were now nearly three years old and like rabbits charging everywhere, and always fighting. They were so competitive and poor Michael always came off worse, as Peter was stronger physically and vocally. However, for a tube of smarties, at almost three years old, they were willingly toilet-trained in two hours!! Easy-peasy – why get hysterical over it. I always believed it wasn't a race to see who was clean first. Have you ever known a child go to school in nappies? Therefore, I remained laid back about it all.

Peter was like a monkey frenetically climbing over and up everything, but he always possessed a disarmingly tantalising smile. Michael was so fat and lazy he couldn't be bothered to walk until he was two years old! He was so cuddly and placid, with a gentle smile; he took in everything that was going on around him. He was very accommodating and accepting, easy to please. However, all four were remarkably well behaved when I was teaching.

I discovered that I would try my hand at entering pupils for Royal College of Music Exams. I couldn't believe that I never had a failure – most of the pupils passed with distinction or merit. I took all the pupils who were capable up to Grade Five. I thoroughly enjoyed starting them off as total beginners. I preferred not to have the stress of teaching beyond Grade Five; I knew where my strengths lay. Two of my pupils went on in later years to train at the Royal College of Music in London. I was very chuffed when their parents phoned to tell me.

The autumn term of 1990 left the school without a music teacher, as she had to move away because of her husband's job. This left the school without a concert for Christmas. As a governor, I felt I had a duty and a skill to offer. I suggested to Jeff that I knocked up something musical for the parents to come and see; I would rather that than offer to do cooking or painting with the children!

Jeff leapt at the idea. After Christmas, I continued to come in on a voluntary basis and give the children guitar lessons, as Chris was learning at the time. During the spring term, Jeff suggested I apply for the music-teaching post.

I couldn't believe what I was hearing!

'I haven't been to university!' I screamed back at him. He told me I could train 'on the job' by being assessed and attending courses.

Jeff was completely convinced I was capable of taking on the job and doing well, not remotely bothered that I had no degree. He said, 'People are born to teach. You can't learn it from a book.' I had to agree with him, but he had much more confidence in me than I did! If I was accepted at the interview – and there were other candidates – then I was now going to do proper teaching – class music and assemblies and so on.

I needed time to think it through. Quickly I arrived at the decision – if Jeff was willing to take me on then who was I to argue. It was stay at home – doing what exactly? – or I could run with this idea and give it a go. Crossroads – what to do?

In the summer term of 1991, the twins started school. I went straight to Jeff's office, where we let out a screech of relief and laughter – phew, I was finally going to have some time on my own.

Wrong! Peter and Michael started school on the Tuesday and I became their music teacher on the Wednesday! They used to refer to me as Mrs Mummy!

It was rather lovely teaching all four of my children music and singing and so forth. It was hard work but I loved it.

During this time, I was voted vice-chairman of governors. I was now wearing so many hats. I was a governor, teacher, parent and friend of the head teacher, who by now had become a close family friend.

I decided the school should put on the musical *Yanomamo*, written by Sting, a vibrant piece. The story was about the Amazon rainforest, and there was a part for every child in the juniors who wanted to be in the play. Everything from animals, birds and fish, to plants, trees, and Indians, of course.

Jeff said he wanted to support me, because this was such a huge undertaking and I was new at the task. He invited me to his house for tea once a week during the planning stage. It was lovely, an old Victorian renovated house in Reading. There was always something going on and there were lodgers and visitors all the time. The atmosphere was so relaxing and easy to be around.

I was very nervous about the production, as it was my first experience. Jeff always encouraged me saying 'trust me, trust me!'

The musical went ahead and was a huge success. The children and parents loved it and my own parents came to see it. Dad was a monetary supporter of the World Wildlife Fund, which included the Yanomamo tribe. We raised a good sum of money for the WWF and I was thrilled I had found the courage months before to face the challenge of school music teacher when I stood at the crossroads. All thanks to Jeff's encouragement and belief in me. I was thankful he had given me a chance and had stuck his neck on the block for me – he had no real proof I would be able to achieve success for the school.

I wasn't being paid much for doing the teaching post, as I was considered a tutor on the payroll and not a teacher although I worked harder than any music teacher, I have met since. Jeff gave me a chance and really got me started in my career. I learnt a lot from him and listened to his advice and guidance. I respected his style and his gentle way with the children and I so wanted to acquire the same skill.

My marriage was beginning to show the strain of many years of struggling, lack of sleep, lack of money, lack of any peace, lack of quality time spent together. Because I was now working and becoming more self-confident, I became less tolerant of certain things I had accepted over time but now found unacceptable. We were arguing more and more, finding it difficult to touch base on anything without there being a disagreement of views. We had obviously grown apart. My doctor was already advising me that my health was suffering because of the strain and tension. I suffered horrendous and regular migraine headaches and dizzy spells, and dramatically lost weight.

Jeff noticed the issues and offered to become my unpaid counsellor – he had a counselling qualification. He said he was very pleased to help and would regularly see me in his office for an hour every Wednesday when I had finished teaching.

Eileen's daughter Rebecca suffered terribly with asthma. This particular day I had received a call to say she was rushed into hospital, the future uncertain. I had to teach that day, but collapsed in a heap and had to go home – the news about Rebecca became a catalyst to face everything in my life I had been hiding from.

During this time, Jeff recommended that I go on retreat to an abbey for some peace. I had never done this before, so I thought I would give it a go. Jeff took me and showed me the ropes. I loved it from the moment I first walked through the door. Ten years on, I still regularly visit. It is a wonderful refuelling experience. I was so grateful to Jeff for introducing me to this side of life. I remain grateful.

My friendship with Jeff extended beyond the school environment. By now I was regularly visiting Jeff's house with the children – having dinner, being invited to parties and barbecues. David would be invited as well. Sometimes, we would be invited to Philip's house, the neighbour I had met the first time I ever socialised with Jeff. Jeff's street held an annual carol-singing evening ending with supper at someone's house in the road. Being a music teacher was helpful, as I had access to song sheets. My children, except Nicola, who was very rarely invited, loved going. My family had become fully accepted by all of Jeff's neighbours; it was understood we spent a lot of time together as good friends and colleagues.

Jeff's friend Brian worked as a chef at a company in Winnersh. It was suggested that the school choir and myself attend the company's staff Christmas lunch, performing Christmas music and singing carols. We all received a free lunch as payment. This became a popular event for all and we were invited back for three years running!

David was always working late and at weekends. It felt as if David was on one team and the children and I were on another going in a different direction. Realising I had begun to feel abandoned, Jeff suggested I might like to team up with him to hear a series of classical concerts held at The Hexagon in Reading. These began as occasional events, but the following year we went to all twelve. Knowing I rarely had a break from the children, Jeff and Brian invited me, with others, on theatre trips to London, which I thoroughly enjoyed. I was now appreciating a life and interests of my own.

During school, there were times when I questioned why it was mainly boys Jeff counselled. He told me that in schools it was mainly boys who had problems with the female teachers and with education generally. He said many female teachers did not know how to get through to boys without being bossy. In some ways, even now, I believe that to be true. He was now also a counsellor for youth within the church community and always took the confirmation classes with the Year Five and Six children.

I decided I needed to extend my teaching hours in schools, reducing the home teaching. I could not take on any more pupils at home – I was full. St Sebastian's school only wanted me one day a week. So I started asking around if there was a school which might need a peripatetic piano teacher. Luckily, the Marist Convent Junior School in Ascot was short of a teacher, so I applied and was immediately employed.

Pupil numbers grew and I was popular with the staff and girls. The head of music for the senior school suggested I might like to take on the recorder groups. My income was now really growing. How far I had come since teaching Rebecca!

Things at home gradually became worse. When my Dad died in the summer of 1994, I knew things were coming to the point of no return. I could feel myself heading for some kind of breakdown. The doctor was very concerned. I could feel another imminent crossroads looming!

During this time, Jeff would offer to take the boys swimming after school with some friends. Chris was now at St Crispin's School in Wokingham and was finding it difficult at home sometimes. Jeff suggested he might like to go to his house for tea sometimes and stay over. Chris had always got on well with Jeff and we agreed it would be a good idea to give him some space away from the home environment.

During half-terms and holidays, it became a regular event for Jeff to take Chris or other boys to London to visit museums or galleries. Sometimes Chris would go alone, sometimes with a friend. All was well; Jeff knew I had little money so he always paid. No need for suspicion, as he was now almost a member of the family, accepted and loved by us all – except Nicky, who could never stand him from the moment she started school. I will explain later. At the time I thought she was jealous of the attention directed at her brothers. In fact, she could be extremely rude to Jeff outside of school, so much so that on one occasion I forced her to write a letter of apology to Jeff. She still remembers that occasion and how she was with him, admitting she was ruder to him than to anyone else she has ever met!

One half-term, he suggested Chris might like to go with a group to Paris on Eurostar. Chris was delighted and appeared to have a great time. However, on his return he seemed reluctant ever to return to Jeff's. I questioned Jeff about it and he replied, 'For goodness sake Marilyn, Chris is now over 14, he has his own life and mates – he doesn't want to hang round at my place any more. He is growing up, it happens.' Not having ever had brothers, and being unfamiliar with teenage-boy behaviour, I accepted the reason and carried on regardless.

I often wondered why Jeff always took boys swimming after school and never the girls. He would say he didn't do 'tits and bits', being a bachelor! The deputy head,

25

Jean, and Jill, his secretary, were always telling him he was unwise to take the children after school with no other adult supervision, or written authority from parents. Most Fridays he would take about four lads off in his car to Coral Reef adventure pool, stopping off for sweets on the way home.

In full view of parents, he would regularly let the lads at school sit behind the wheel of his car and let them steer it around the playground. Everyone thought he was a cool headmaster and laughed it off. No one suspected he may have a sinister side to him.

Jill and Jean would often warn him about shutting his office door when he had boys in his office. However, he continued to do so. He explained to her (as he pointed to the picture which hung on his study wall) that Jesus was his judge, that everything he did he talked to God about and that others did not have the same view of life and living. Every morning before school, you could find him in the church praying for half an hour before the school bell would ring. All the staff and parents thought he was such a deeply religious man.

Sometimes, the subject would come up in the staff room of Jeff being single. He always said he didn't feel relaxed about commitment and anyway he had a low sex drive. Therefore, marriage never bothered him and anyway he now considered himself to be too old and of no use to anybody.

In his thirties, he had become friendly with a woman called Sue who was widowed and had two young boys. He met her at a church in Reading and helped her with her sons, as they were apparently difficult to handle. At the time friends thought he would marry her, but he left her to train as a monk, to test his faith and where he was going with it. After a few months, he left the monastery and to my knowledge, he didn't return to the relationship and she married another man.

I was music teacher at the school for six years, but left to take up another more lucrative post at a pre-prep school in Binfield whilst continuing to teach at the Marist Convent.

David and I had attended counselling sessions at the surgery, and for a time I was hopeful we would overcome our problems and all would be well. However, the sessions helped me enormously, and I began to change and see things differently. I realised I was entitled to claiming a life for myself. I was right to seek ways of entertaining myself. It didn't make me a bad mother. It was OK to think and feel the way I did about some things in life. I had a right to an opinion. I had a right to expect physical support from my husband when things at home with the children were tough – I was exhausted. My father had died, and I wasn't being unreasonable to want an empathic and sensitive shoulder to lean on. David would often say, 'You are a Hawes woman and therefore have to be tough – Hawes men don't do tears!' I felt unloved, lonely and unaccepted. Although I knew David loved me, in the end I couldn't feel it. I had lost my self-worth.

Over time, years in fact, Jeff had begun to fill that gap, in a close, platonic way. Of course he did. Like an animal watching its prey. He watched opportunities develop, worming his way into the cracks and gaps. It is called grooming!

He made me feel worthy and loved. He helped me heal and made life fun again. Sex and being in love never entered into the equation. Had they done so, I would have run like a scared rabbit.

In hindsight I suppose David might like to say, 'Ah, so it was Jeff's fault we got divorced!' That isn't true.

27

Jeff actually made it bearable to stay longer than I did. I had become dysfunctional within myself.

At this time, a year after my father died, I started divorce proceedings. I felt I had let my father down. However, my mum told me had Dad lived he would not have been surprised. She said he was always telling her that one day he was certain I would up sticks and go. He used to say to Mum that he knew I was struggling; I had stopped smiling with my eyes, merely going through the motions. He knew there were deep problems but never voiced them to me.

The divorce went through but the sale of the house was much more difficult. David and I lived on in the same house, although already divorced, for about 18 months. It was a terrible time for everyone; I was sleeping on a camp bed in a different bedroom until we finally moved out. I thought I would lose my mind if I stayed in the house any longer. I asked my lawyer if it was all right for me to move out. He said 'No!' but I did so anyway. Not to do so at the time would have brought on a nervous breakdown. I refused to risk my health because of the law!

I was facing another crossroads not for the first time in my life, nor the last! Another leap of faith into the unknown. Not having anywhere to go and finding the cost of renting too expensive, Jeff suggested he look after the twins while I moved in with a female colleague from the Marist Convent together with Chris and Nicky. My friend Carol and her girls disrupted their life for us. We all thought she was only taking us in for a few weeks until the house sale and purchase had gone through. As with all house moves, nothing is simple and in the end we were in this situation for five months.

Carol had divorced a few years earlier for similar reasons to myself. One Sunday morning she rang and told me that she and her girls had decided we were to stay with them if we became desperate. She handed me the keys to her house and one night we turned up with endless bin liners of belongings. I slept with Nicky in Carol's bed. Carol moved into her daughter's room, as Gaynor was at university. Chris slept in Beth's room, as she was away. When Gaynor returned from university, she slept on the living-room sofa. Amy was the only one who stayed where she should! Loaning Nicky nail varnish and make-up. Funnily enough, it was a very special and humorous time. We had wonderful, mind-stretching conversations. We never once fell out, although, if Carol is honest, I think the endless phone ringing drove her mad! I love this family with all my heart, and owe them so much. They are very special people, and such a selfless act of friendship makes Carol truly the Good Samaritan.

One morning I nearly set light to the street by exploding Carol's toaster. We could both hardly breathe and ran into the street with hardly a stitch on to escape the fumes. All day at school, Carol and I stank of burnt toast. No amount of perfume would disguise it!

Bathroom patrol in the mornings was hilarious. We were all given strict time zones. I discovered Nicky chatted in her sleep. One morning while still asleep, she urged me to get up, as it was quarter past six in the morning – my bathroom slot. Thinking it was dark but taking little notice, I showered, washed my hair, put on my make-up. The light hadn't improved, hardly surprising as I discovered the time was actually half past three in the morning. All made-up and ready for the day, I climbed back into bed. Her ladyship was sleeping soundly, unaware of the chaos she had created!

Locking up at night was a nightmare. With so many of us coming and going late into the night, we could never be sure who had come home. Carol and I established a register – as only teachers can! As you came in you had to tick your box. All went well until weekends, when most came home less than sober and ticked the wrong name, or two names. People were still locked out. One night Chris was the last and he slept downstairs. Unable to wake anyone, he threw stones up at the window, he assumed in his stupor, of what was my room. However, poor Carol was the victim having to stagger out in the dark, while the rest of us slept on.

I would travel over to see the boys after work at Jeff's house and stay for dinner before returning to Carol's house in Wokingham. Jeff and I would often still go to the Hexagon in Reading to hear classical concerts or go to a show in London with other friends as well. It was so lovely to have a caring platonic male friend. Having got divorced there was nothing more I wanted or needed from a relationship than pure friendship. I had never had a male friend like him and we all thought the world of him. Friends would say, 'Jeff clearly adores you and your family. Does he never make a move, hold your hand or anything?'

I was horrified. How could people think that way? We had a beautiful friendship. But my mother was less than relaxed about it all. She felt certain Jeff was going to make a move toward me now that I was single. Why else was he paying the children and me so much attention? She said, 'I may be 70, darling, but I am not stupid – what he is offering you is way beyond the call of friendship!'

I was cross with her. Although I wasn't needy, I needed his friendship and cherished it. I felt privileged to have him as my friend – someone who liked me just for me, who wasn't a threat. As I said earlier, I had begun to think he was a celibate gay, and so what if he was – it didn't make him a paedophile. Jeff was deeply religious and pure – sex was something I never linked to him, and sex outside marriage would have gone against his beliefs, whether he was gay or straight.

Jeff would buy the boys clothes, shoes, games and toys even taking them away on holiday with a friend of his to Padstow, as I was unable to pay for a holiday. He took them several times. I do remember contributing some of the cost however. To keep down the expense, they all shared a family room at the hotel in which they stayed. I trusted him completely, and another adult was present.

I could not keep accepting this level of generosity and support. I even asked him to stop, as I knew it would be impossible to maintain when I moved into my house and I was becoming nervous that the boys might not want to return home to stay with me and Chris and Nicky.

One evening we decided to pay a surprise visit to the boys at Jeff's. The three of us had hit a low and were really missing the boys. We arrived at Jeff's unexpectedly and uninvited, and we were given something of a frosty and stern welcome. Peter and Michael were thrilled to see us and we spent the evening together. Before we left, I was upstairs and Jeff came up to explain it wasn't convenient to pop in as I had. I thought it odd but put it down to him being a fussy bachelor who liked things to be organised and pre-arranged.

On another occasion, I took the boys out to Henley on my own for a Sunday afternoon to play on the green, have a picnic and watch the world go by. We spent ages there and on my return Jeff was, in a way, possessive, questioning why I had been so long. Odd,

31

yes, but I put it down to natural concern and the fact that he knew that the boys living at his home was going to end in a few weeks. This maybe was his knee-jerk response to realising that the situation was only temporary. He even told me and the boys that he had included them in his will.

With the benefit of hindsight, people now say to me, 'Did you never think it odd that the headmaster offered to have pupils (meaning the twins) stay with him?' Why would I? It wasn't like that. He had been a family friend to us all for years. It was a small school with an intimate, friendly, very special atmosphere and ethos of love and caring. That is what made the school and Jeff so admired, loved and respected. To be honest, I thought he was enjoying being able to be a caring surrogate grandparent as he had missed out on being a dad, and it was lovely to watch him enjoy their company, providing him with a temporary family life.

I am not a possessive person. I have always believed children are on loan to you and then you let them go. If any of my children can spread some happiness into someone else's life then so be it. After all, I had struggled to have children, so I knew the heartache when it doesn't happen. I felt comfortable with the arrangement.

After four months of being separated from the twins, I could take no more. We all wanted to be reunited as a family. We had been patient long enough and my house purchase was being held up because the court settlement had not been resolved, or even heard.

One day, I stormed into my lawyer's office. I insisted he get all of us rehoused so we could once again be a family. I told him the courts in this land are supposed to be proactive with family support, and to get me rehoused so that I could get my children back! I was told it was impossible to rush these things. I was very frank with him and said, 'Fine, they can't rush these things. It has been four months – how long does it take, for goodness sake? – I will go to the court myself and, if necessary, get arrested so that someone will be forced to hear me!' And I walked out, leaving him stunned and open-mouthed. Where had the broken, distraught woman he knew disappeared to? I refused to take no for an answer.

The following day the lawyer leapt into action. Having told me this had never been achieved before, I found myself with a court settlement in my hand seven days later! Judge Jolly, bless him, moved heaven and earth to hear my case. He was horrified I had been overlooked. As we left the court, my lawyer said, 'Well, that's a first. I have never pushed the courts to act before. So, it can be done, obviously!'

Finally, I moved into my house in August 1997 with Chris and Nicky. Peter and Michael were away again on holiday with Jeff and his friend. Chris helped me to decorate the boys' room and there was energy and excitement all around. I was conscious that the boys would find it strange being back with us, and, seeing as they had experienced so many treats at Jeff's, I decided to invest in cable TV. Peter and Michael moved back in with us. All their friends helped us move in and we had great times and much laughter in that house. I decided to live alongside the children more as a student than a mum, as I wanted to feel bonded with them and understand their way of life. The house was always full of laughter and full of divorced friends and teenagers – I loved it. I felt young again and life was fun – penniless, but fun!

Jeff told me the boys felt they wanted some 'de-twinning time', some quality time with me on the basis that the other twin brother was not there. I bought into this, as it seemed a good idea. So sometimes I had Peter to myself and at other times Michael. I was so busy working long hours, I liked the idea of spending a calmer time with each of them, as they were always at each other's throats. Jeff explained that this was because they were teenage boys sharing a small bedroom.

After two or three occasions on Michael's return, he was unbearable. His behaviour was explosively violent and the way he spoke to me was unacceptable. At one stage, he was so bad I rang his dad to come and take Michael away to stay with him for a couple of days until he sorted his brain out!

Eventually, after the third occasion, I rang Jeff and told him that I could no longer support the idea of Michael staying over. I was sure he was overly enjoying the attention and reacting on his return home, as I was unable to offer the same input, having four children to cope with. For a nanosecond I found myself thinking, 'This behaviour is typical – when a child has been abused.' I immediately dismissed the thought and chastised myself for thinking such wicked things.

Jeff explained: 'Marilyn, I always told you Michael was the quieter, more sensitive child, not made of rubber like Peter. He was bound to be the one who took the divorce badly, conscious there was no father figure in the house, making him feel his family was dysfunctional. Send him over and I will talk to him for you.'

And so I did. It made sense, didn't it?

A close friend, Heather, was round one day when Jeff popped in. While I was in another room, she was uneasy at the way Jeff called for Michael and pulled him onto his lap. She asked me after he had gone how I felt about it. I replied: 'What are you trying to say?

34

Jeff has been around the boys since they were tiny tots. He's always got children on his lap – he's part of the family. I am used to seeing him cuddling kids – what is wrong with you?'

After a year, Chris went off to Bristol University and I missed him so much. There was this awful empty feeling inside for a while. He had been such a support to me, but he had to get on with his life.

That November I had an operation on my throat. I had over the months, following the stress of the divorce, developed a croaky, husky voice and had become unable to sing. Teaching was a nightmare; others had to sing for me. It was discovered I had large nodules on the vocal chords.

My mum came and looked after me for a week or so – I was unable to talk for weeks! Jeff would visit, never really talking to her. She voiced her opinion to me. 'I can't work out why he won't look me in the eye, Marilyn.' I just shrugged my shoulders. My throat was agony; how was I ever going to do my job as a music teacher? I had other worries right then!

Chris would often come home or we would travel to see him but after he had been away for a year I wanted something more and different. I realised I could not live like this forever – the children were getting older and I had to find a life of my own outside and separate from theirs. I didn't want them to feel I was dependent on their company.

The hardest part of being a parent is 'letting go', giving your child the space to develop their own ideas about how they see their life going forward. Allowing them to make mistakes as being the only way to learn about life. It is a necessary part of real parenting, but one I have always found to be a tough wrench on the heartstrings.

How was I going to change my life? I toyed around with an idea. I had always followed my lovely friend's advice. Sister Olivia always said to me, 'To change is to grow, and to grow is to change frequently.' Taken literally, that meant I should now be twelve feet tall!

My dad could never quite accept my ability to change tack – he questioned my 'stickability'. I would say, 'Versatility is the word you need, Daddy dear!' And we would both laugh.

So it was time to move on again.

4

New Horizons

New Year's Eve 1998 we spent at Jeff's house, as we had every year for several years. He always made such an enormous effort. Christmas was also very special there, but I love having family Christmases at home with me and mine, and so we would be invited to him for the New Year and Jeff would visit us on Christmas day at our new house.

Lots of friends and family would be invited, even the lodgers. Everyone made a supreme effort to 'scrub up well' – bow ties and evening dresses. The table was an eye-popper every time. Jeff was immensely artistic with design and no one saw the table until we were about to eat. The table would take him virtually all day the day before to dress. Candles, serviettes and decorations were coordinated and there was a new theme and colour every year. The table's centre decoration was a work of art. He would hide within the arrangement chocolate liqueurs and all sorts of gifts for the guests. The menu would be inscribed in beautiful handwriting for each table place and the seating carefully thought through.

The children and I always enjoyed the time there. However, this year I sat thinking, 'What am I doing here? I am in my forties and I am spending New Year's Eve with friends in their late fifties up to their eighties.'

37

There is absolutely nothing wrong with that, except I have always loved New Year's Eve; it is a great time to reflect, put things behind you and happily look forward to the year ahead. And also to celebrate, drink, eat and dance and be generally raucous for one night of the year. Suddenly, being at Jeff's wasn't enough and I sensed a strange atmosphere that night. I felt odd being there – I had no idea why.

I returned home knowing this year I had to seek something new. I rang my Aunt and discussed my predicament with her. I had shown no interest in men for two or three years, but I could feel that I wanted to dress up for an evening out again, with someone other than divorced girlfriends. I was obviously recovering from the effect of the divorce. I like male company and was clearly now missing the banter and conversation, and some romance.

At three in the morning on 3rd January 1998, I crept out of bed and found the Yellow Pages and went to the page for introduction agencies. I remember discussing it with myself.

'I can't do this, can I?'

'Why not? What do you have to lose? You are never going to meet anyone teaching at a convent school or in a pre-prep!'

'What would Mum say?'

'Why tell her?'

'How about my friends – what would they think?'

'Why tell them? Who needs to know?'

'What would the children think? I should tell them.'

'Yes, but they are always saying you should get out and have a laugh with new people!'

So I shut me eyes and circled my finger over the page and with my eyes still closed I chose a space on the page. On opening my eyes I saw that I had found the number for Elite, so at three-thirty I rang and left a message. I said, 'If you don't phone me back I will never have the guts to do this again!'

The following day, I received a call and a meeting was arranged at my home. Chris and Nicky thought it was a great idea. They were concerned I might start going through the lonely-hearts page, so this felt safer to them!

The letters, which were similar to CVs began to arrive. Nicky loved reading them and trying to imagine what the guys would be like. I had a great time and met some interesting people.

I decided not to tell Jeff. He was happily having the boys some weekends, so if I met someone I could go out on a Saturday night and the boys needn't feel insecure or worry about it. They were now twelve or thirteen.

On Saturday 4th April 1998, I met Roger. By now I had become used to meeting men by arrangement, in a pub or bar. He kindly offered to meet me in a hotel around the corner from where I lived. He lived at Canary Wharf, but did not want me to travel too far. I was already impressed – what a gentleman!

We had spoken for an hour or two on the phone. He had described what he would be wearing. I was reading the menu and it was about eight o'clock. A man walked in wearing a blue blazer and a salmon-pink shirt as described by Roger. I looked up and said, 'Hi, I'm Marilyn.'

The man said, 'Nice to meet you – I am with my wife over there.'

I wanted the floor to swallow me – my face was burning red and I was wearing a red silk blouse. The colour clash was hideous.

After ten minutes from underneath my menu, I saw

a pair of shoes. I was too nervous to speak but Roger did that for me. To my mind, he was the image of Clive James!

I immediately liked him. He had a lovely Northern accent and a real masculinity about him – I already felt safe with him.

When I was growing up nobody told me that masculinity is something more than just being a man. It is about accountability, responsibility and a total feeling of care and protection – a bit like what is expected of a knight! Roger had this quality.

We went out for a meal and had a great evening. Roger came back for coffee and *Match of the Day* was on. I couldn't believe that I appeared to have clicked with a football fan – I hate the game unless England are playing.

Chris came home and the two of them were talking football. I remember Roger showing Chris in my small living room how Brazilians pass the ball.

I eventually told my mum I had found an OK guy, and that Chris and Nicky both liked him. She advised me not to say anything to Jeff as she felt immediately he knew my support network would be withdrawn. Having a real man in my life she did not believe was in his scheme of things. She was also naturally nervous, being my mum, about me having a romance. She was anxious that I hold on to my life as it was, having just got things sorted.

Roger was everything I said I would never marry. He was from the North. I had always liked soft southerners and his humour was almost brutal at times, even rude. He had been in the navy – use your imagination there! He had charm, but he certainly wasn't one of life's charmers! He had divorced eleven years earlier, and had been out with more than a few younger women. He did, however, have four children of his own, so he knew exactly about family dynamics. He knew how to look after a family.

Time went on and the relationship really developed, and the children all liked him, which mattered enormously. He would ring at the most horrendous hour of the night to speak to me – it drove Chris nuts, as he was sleeping in the room above. My bedroom was a converted dining room below, so he could hear the laughter at three in the morning. Anyway, Roger could never accept my friendship with Jeff.

It really annoyed me. He kept implying that Jeff was after children not women. I should explain that Roger is a qualified behavioural analyst. Using that knowledge he would explain his thoughts. I was furious and we would often fiercely argue about it. I constantly said, 'Roger, you are one of those hundreds of men who are incapable of believing men and women can be platonic. You know nothing about him and I won't have a word said against him. He has been close to my family for years, is a thoroughly good man, very religious, with his heart in the right place. You have never met him, you know nothing about the man – so be quiet!' I would not have a word said against my friend.

At dinner parties or evenings in the pub, Roger would feel compelled to say, 'What do you think of Jeff, then?' And I would send a resounding kick from under the table. But he would not let it drop. He refused to take No for an answer!

By now, Jeff was aware I had a boyfriend and seemed to be pleased for me, telling me he always knew that one day I would find someone. I was relieved.

In June 1999, I needed an emergency hysterectomy. I was Jeff's closest friend and yet he only visited me once and for a short time. He lived only around the corner from the BUPA hospital. Brian, also my friend, never visited me at all, which was very hurtful.

Overnight my music-teaching career in schools ended, without me having the chance to say goodbye. I was distraught – this job had given me back my life and a means to setting up my own home and moving my life on. It was my best friend. I had become a teacher without having worked for a degree. I wanted to write to the nuns who once taught me, to tell them, 'Hey, I did it anyway!'

Roger had suggested that we might move over to San Francisco, as he had lived there before and thought we would all love the life. When I mentioned it to a friend of Jeff's, he said to me, 'What will Jeff do? Will you take the boys?'

I was shocked, and found myself saying, 'The boys are not *his*, they are my sons. I truly appreciate all he has done for them and for me, but he mustn't become possessive of them!'

I failed to tell Roger, as I didn't want another debate about Jeff.

In July, before we moved away, Jeff invited the boys and me over for tea to see his new house. They had moved from the lovely Victorian house to a smaller, more modern one near Tadley. Roger was not invited – he was furious, and insisted he was coming with us. He, after all, was taking on the responsibility of my family and me, and he refused to be excluded. Anyway, it was his chance finally to meet this friend of mine!

We arrived with a magnum of champagne. We sat in the lounge chatting. All was going well. Jeff and Roger faced each other across the room like sparring partners in the ring! We were shown around the house. Roger noticed Jeff place Michael on his lap – Michael was now thirteen. He placed him on his lap with Michael's back against Jeff's stomach. He then laid Michael across his lap and began stroking Michael's back right to the waistline of his shorts.

Roger froze. I noticed Peter throw a look at Roger. Roger leapt up, saying, 'We are going now!' To my mind we had only just arrived.

He immediately quizzed Peter as to where Michael had suddenly disappeared. Peter said, 'He has gone upstairs with Jeff.'

Roger ran up the stairs two at a time yelling for Michael to come downstairs *now*!

Michael appeared with a £10 note in his hand, which he said he had been given as pocket money for his holiday. Peter was then given some money downstairs.

Roger bundled us in the car and as soon as the boys were asleep said to me, 'Those lads are *never* spending time with that man again – do you understand?'

I was totally silent – I didn't understand what had happened. Roger said he would explain later. When we arrived home, Roger told me how a man should place a child on a lap, and, at 13 years old you don't even go there!

Jeff rang the next day telling me he didn't think Roger was the sort of man he could befriend. I replied that he needn't worry, because the feeling was mutual on Roger's part as well.

A week or so later, Roger arrived home from work. He heard Michael on the phone to Jeff. Roger came through to the kitchen and my friend Eileen was with me. 'You girls come with me *now* – we are going to the pub! Don't ask questions – get in the car!'

Whatever could have happened? He was livid. We sat down. 'Marilyn, take off your rose-tinted glasses! Is it normal for a 13-year-old boy to be encouraged by a 63-year-old man to say, "Yes, I love you too?!" That is the conversation I have just heard! Eileen, you tell her – you are their godmother!'

Eileen explained that until now she had found Roger's comments difficult to take. However, as their godmother and my close friend she urged me it might now be advisable to be aware, just in case Roger's suspicions were accurate. I was numb. I couldn't believe what I was being asked to consider.

In August 1999 Roger and I decided to move to Billingshurst. We had seen the identical house being built in Wokingham which was £150,000 cheaper in West Sussex.

If Roger was correct with his thoughts about Jeff, it crossed my mind that Jeff would try to see the boys through their father when they visited him. We met with David to alert him. Roger explained his concerns and the reasons why he had them. Me? I was still bewildered.

We decided to face new horizons and a fresh future. Chris was still at university. Nicky had taken her GCSEs and was due to start in the sixth form, and the boys were about to go into Year 9 and, therefore, at that stage had not even chosen their options. It seemed a great window in time – if there is such a time, when you can disrupt and move a family who have lived and grown up in the same town all their lives. I had lived in Wokingham for 21 years.

All my friends wished me well. Although they liked Roger enormously, they were concerned – I was with a man I had met through an introduction agency. On 29th April 2000, Roger and I married and I became Mrs Woods.

We must have invited 140 friends and family. Everyone came – except Jeff. I was so upset, as were the boys.

Why wouldn't my long-time and closest, most supportive male friend not want to see me married and leading a happy, normal, secure life at last? Why wouldn't he want to see the boys he had helped so much looking great, happy and healthy?

He rang me the morning of the wedding to wish me well, saying he just didn't like weddings – he would rather attend funerals because a funeral is permanent!

I decided jealousy was indeed a terrible sin, like a cancer eating away at you. I never thought Jeff was jealous of Roger being the man in my life, only that it meant Roger was now their stepdad and Jeff had to step down. But why couldn't he still be a friend?

From that time on I occasionally wrote to him, but we mainly heard from him on birthdays, at Easter and Christmas. Personal contact with the boys had ceased – or so I thought!

In the summer of 2001, Jeff and I met up for the first time since that night at his new house. We spent the day at Wisley Gardens. I explained to Roger that I wanted to meet him for old times sake. Roger understood, or certainly appeared to do so.

I asked Jeff why he had decided not to attend our wedding. He explained he felt it would be difficult for Roger. In his opinion, Roger may have found it too much seeing a man at the wedding who had played such a large part in our lives over the years, a man who had been instrumental in helping me with the boys. I told Jeff that Roger was more of a man than that! Jeff showed very little interest in the wedding photos.

After that, conversations regarding Jeff became a rare event. Roger decided to lay off, but he did say to me, 'One day, darling, the door bell or the phone will ring and you will find the police on the doorstep – I am sure I am right but I hope for your sake I am wrong.'

5

2002 – Mum's Gap Year

Life settled down in Billingshurst and after a while I became used to not teaching. I couldn't decide what I wanted to do. We had moved into a new house that constantly needed the attention of the builders, as the snag list never seemed to end. There didn't seem time to work. It was lovely to be there for the children. I felt I had missed out when I was having to work such long hours, and I enjoyed being there for them when they came in from school, even though they were older. I loved to chat and laugh with them, hearing about their day.

The boys loved the new school, The Weald in Billingshurst, and found it to be more advanced than their previous one. They began to make many friends, who now use our home as the alternative sixth-form common room!

I became involved with the village church and started up a percussion group for the church to encourage youngsters. For my part, I gave my time voluntarily. I would hold a two-hour music session on the first Saturday of the month – any child could come. I taught music for the first hour and we would accompany the following day's hymns for the children's service in the second hour. The group grew and some of the children

47

became confirmed and joined the junior choir, and we kept gaining new recruits. We became popular enough to be requested to attend certain services!

The boys would see their dad and we would drop off and collect according to arrangements. All was well.

In January 2002, Chris announced, although I had known it was imminent, that he would be leaving on his world travels within two weeks with a university mate. Although I knew I would miss him, I was so pleased he was getting on with his life. So off we went to Heathrow to see him off. I couldn't believe how sad I felt and yet happy. I would not see him again until 2nd August that year.

Ten days later, on 9th February 2002, Nicky was off on her travels. She had planned to travel with her boyfriend of two years, but the relationship went wrong a week or so before she left for Bali. She announced that she was going to go anyway. I was horrified! Nicky is drop-dead gorgeous, she has a wicked sense of humour and she was bound to be the prey of every male. I said, 'No, Nicky, you can't go! Please don't go, it is dangerous!'

Being *my* daughter, I should have known the reply would be, 'Mum, I'm going. I can always come back on the next plane if I don't like it!'

Roger and I bought her an all-singing, all-dancing mobile phone so she could call us any time from anywhere, and I made her promise to keep in regular contact.

So back we went to Heathrow – again! I was inconsolable. Both my children within a short time had walked into their new life with my blessing. I couldn't hide my tears. I felt a mix of admiration and joy for them. It was the pain of 'letting go' again. I had to be strong.

As I waved goodbye to Nicky and watched her walk to departures, I had this eerie feeling that for her something was going to go wrong! I have always been a touch psychic.

Having a new house, there was a bare garden to plan and plant. My Dad would be amazed to see what I have achieved, never having been interested in gardening before. He was there on my shoulder, showing me what to do. In the last two years, I have found gardening to be the only grounding thing, something which still makes sense when nothing else in life does! It is uncomplicated, the plants don't answer back, you plant them and they grow if you care for them or die if you don't. They come and go with the seasons. I found myself planting a garden bed for Chris and one for Nicky, completely unaware of what I was doing until I had done it. Whilst planting each bed I was consumed by thoughts of them. I would look at the moon at night and say, 'Goodnight.' Wherever they were in the world, they were looking at the same moon. It was a cosmic communication.

At this time, I had begun working in the curriculum support department at The Weald School. Since I was a young child, I have always had a deep sense of care for less-able people – be they babies, children or adults and also for animals. Animals are completely vulnerable.

We regularly had emails from the children and Nicky was very good at phoning. Then it happened.

At five in the morning one Tuesday the phone rang and I knew it was going to be my worst nightmare. Nicky was explaining to Roger she had fallen on a boat on the Great Barrier Reef. I froze – this was what I had dreaded since she left the country.

Roger told me he thought she had ruptured a kidney, as it sounded very similar to accidents he had witnessed on the rugby pitch.

49

Her phone went dead and we had no idea which hospital she was being taken to. I had to go to work at the school, having told Roger I would be getting the next plane to Australia if this proved to be critical. Roger spent ages phoning hospitals near Airlie Beach and the surrounding Queensland area, trying to track down Nicky.

After several hours, Roger and the insurance company eventually traced her and I received a call telling me Nicky was critically ill, having completely shattered her kidney, and was too unstable to be flown to a renal unit.

I knew I was on my way to Australia and *nothing* was going to stop me. I told the school I was going, with no idea when, or if, I would be returning.

This could not have come at a worse time, as Peter and Michael were about to sit their GCSEs. Chris was already travelling and was now in New Zealand. Roger said immediately that he was coming with me.

I had become friendly with the wife of a work contact of Roger's. We had arranged the week before to have lunch together, which now happened to be the day I was flying to Australia. We sat in the pub anyway, complaining at the hairs in our salad – in the scheme of things did they matter when my daughter was near to death? How do you spend the time waiting and staying sane? Lynn and her husband Jim, and several close friends, were the most amazing support while we were in Australia, emailing day and night.

Just before we left the country, Nicky's renal consultant informed us that her condition had worsened. They had to operate – if they didn't she would die, and if they did she still might die if they could not stop the bleeding. They would let us know the outcome within six hours or so. We would already be flying by then.

All through the journey I was willing her to live – hang on, Nicky, we're on our way, stick with us.

Thirty hours of flying and time lags later, we arrived at Townsville General Hospital, Queensland. She was in a desperate condition and had a punctured lung. I will never forget for the rest of my life how I felt the moment I saw her. Relief, certainly – she was alive. However, she was connected to masks, drips and cylinders. Bless her. My heart almost stopped. My beautiful, vibrant, smiling daughter had become a skeleton. She looked as though she had aged 30 years.

Nicky displayed enormous courage, always smiling. She never once complained, and showed the same refusal to give in, like her mum. We were enormously proud of her. Her dreams of completing her travels were brought to a dramatic end – she would eventually be coming back to England with me.

After ten days, we were decamped into a superb serviced apartment. Roger had to then go on to Singapore on business, so Nicky and I lived for four weeks in Queensland until she was well enough to travel home.

We actually had a great time; to say we have become intensely bonded would be an understatement. We laughed together, cried together, walked together, ate together; we went everywhere together – joined at the hip.

Friends in England were emailing all the time – when we woke and when we went to bed people had sent messages, flowers, virtual flowers, or had phoned.

One day I was sunbathing on the balcony while Nicky slept, and I watched a rose unfurl. There is something very special at the stage where the bud begins to open just before it is in full bloom. It reminded me of youth and puberty moving into adulthood. Nature was so fascinating.

I sent many letters to friends and family back home to pass the time while Nicky slept and rested.

On our return in early June, I was surprised Jeff hadn't responded to my letter from Australia. I knew he had found Nicky difficult in the past, but surely having been so near to death he would show concern for her and for our family, especially the boys – she was their sister, and they were in the middle of their exams when it happened.

Nicky spent the time quietly at home, becoming increasingly bored. Mentally she wanted to be at work but she tired easily. I wanted to be sure she would be fit to start her university life at Durham in the coming October.

Within a week of returning, I was hit by the stress and anxiety I had felt for Nicky and the relief of being back home with my friends and family. I could not stop shaking, I was unable to sleep and the reality of it all was now affecting my health. In Australia, the doctors often commented on how calm I was. I explained that I was there to get my daughter better and there was no point in my crying and getting hysterical – it wouldn't change or help anything. Anyway, I went to see my doctor and was immediately put on all sorts of pills to calm my blood pressure and adrenalin, and signed off work for the significant future. The doctor also suggested I see a counsellor to talk through my thoughts, fears and feelings for Nicky's life going forward. My name was placed on the waiting list.

Unexpectedly, in late July I received a call from Jeff. The conversation was very odd: 'Hi Marilyn, it's me. How are you?' We chatted briefly about Nicky, and then he said, 'Your voice sounds OK.' I thought why wouldn't it? 'Is that Roger in the distance? Nice to hear him.' Jeff's voice seemed strange.

We then arranged to meet up again at Wisley Gardens in the coming October after Nicky had started university.

Later in the week, I rang Jill and said I had received a very strange call from Jeff. She confirmed having received an identical call, in which he commented on her voice and how OK she sounded. I asked Jill, in her opinion, what did she think was going on in his life? Jill briefly explained I should expect a call from Thames Valley Police some day soon, she couldn't state the reason. Apparently, the police had wanted to see me during the time I was in Australia. She had told them they would have to wait. Recently, they had rung her again and this time they needed my number. I was to expect a call after my holiday.

In early August, Roger, the boys and myself went to San Diego. We had already booked the holiday earlier in the year. Nicky insisted we went and had a break, and Chris had now arrived home from his travels round the world and was there to look out for her. I felt it incredibly difficult to leave Nicky for the first time since her accident, and I missed her dreadfully.

While we were away, nearly every day I said to Roger, 'What on earth do you think the police want?'

He replied, 'I think I know. I hope I am wrong, but I have a hunch I may be right.'

Could it be possible I was on the brink of facing realisation?

6

Realisation

On our return, sure enough, the call came from an officer in the Child Protection Unit of Thames Valley Police. She had permission from West Sussex Police to come and see me, even though it would normally be the remit of police where you live. She explained that because she had been investigating something over a long period it was more appropriate for Thames Valley to handle things.

A date was arranged for Thursday of the following week. She lightly touched on the subject of her visit and we were told that in *no* circumstances were we to speak to the children. So, we continued with the strain of secrecy for about ten days. I couldn't eat and I couldn't sleep. I found it impossible to stay emotionally level, trying not to disclose anything to the boys through my behaviour.

The day came with instructions to the boys that they were to come home directly from school without any mates in tow, and this was very important.

The Child Protection Officer arrived at 12 noon and we were interviewed. I could not believe what I was hearing: 'Marilyn, we are here to ask you questions about Jeff Carney. We understand you have known him for many years as a close friend and colleague. We know he helped look after your children while you were going through a divorce and we have been investigating allegations of child abuse against him.'

I could hardly breathe. My world momentarily stopped moving. What was happening? What was this woman saying to me? How dare she say such things? Who was she to say these things about a man I knew to be such a wonderful friend and a good person?

The realisation hit me – she was going to have to interview the boys! How would they cope with this news of such allegations? They had so much affection and respect for Jeff, so many happy memories of times spent together – this would turn their world upside down, especially as they had only just recovered from the shock of Nicky's accident.

What did the police want from me? What was I expected to say to them? I had nothing to tell them – did I?

Roger stood still, looking at me – his prophecy had come true! I remember that he simply went out to the kitchen and made a cup of tea. I remember thinking, 'How British!'

Then the CPO was looking at me. Was there anything I could remember or had seen which would suggest inappropriate behaviour? Was there anything, given what I now knew about the investigation, which could be taken differently?

I just stared at her. Slowly and reluctantly, I was being forced to examine nanoseconds of information over a 21-year period that I had possibly missed or misread as innocent at the time.

I felt horrible. I wanted to be sick. I felt I was betraying my friend just having to think that way without even speaking my thoughts. I wanted to run away and never come back. I couldn't take this on top of the year I had already experienced – it was too much to bear.

After a while, I began to remember things. This was going to take ages.

There had been a moment several years back, shortly after I divorced. We had all gone to a west country Cathedral to see a youth orchestra perform. We knew a lad who was playing in the orchestra. I went shopping with his mum while the rehearsal took place. It was a boiling-hot summer afternoon and so I decided I would go back to the cathedral in the cool and sit and listen to the rehearsal.

Being a music teacher, I have always been intrigued at how many notches of improvement happen from the last rehearsal to the actual performance. The sense of occasion has a magical effect on everyone, and to witness that difference is fascinating to me.

I went into the cathedral. Jeff was nowhere to be seen. Suddenly, I saw him across the other side by a pillar. Not wanting to disrupt the orchestra, I walked down the side aisle, across the back of the church and silently walked up behind him. He appeared to be hiding behind a pillar. I saw his face and I felt chilled – he was completely lost on another plane, looking dreamily at the right-hand side of the players. I followed his eye line; he seemed to be entranced by one of the children – this boy was blond and the sun beaming through the stained-glass window was casting rainbow colours on his hair. I suddenly realised Jeff was staring at the son of the mother whom I had just left shopping.

I tapped Jeff on the shoulder. He almost jumped from his skin and I asked, 'What are you doing? Why are you hiding behind a pillar?'

He replied, 'I am blown away by the talent of these youngsters and thought it best not to be too visible in case I distracted them. Aren't they amazing – I am so looking forward to the performance tonight. Come on, let's get an ice cream.'

I felt so ashamed; for a nanosecond I imagined he had been leering at this 13-year-old lad. I felt disgusted with myself. I thought, 'Marilyn, you are wicked and evil – stop it right now!' However, just for the record, years later, through the Court of Appeal, I realised that this boy became a victim of Jeff's abuse.

Returning my thoughts to the CPO, I asked her if this was the type of relevant information she was seeking from me. She confirmed my worst thoughts.

I had no choice – anything in the past, over 21 years, which I had discounted as odd and had justified to myself now had to be told officially to the police. I began to realise that the boys Jeff took under his wing were nearly always blond or fair-haired. Invariably most of them had been through or were going through a difficult time. Then I remembered the rose I sat and watched in Australia, and it all became revoltingly clear.

I wondered whether Jeff could possibly be attracted to the 'opening bud' stage in a child's life. In my opinion, he had always had a thing about angelic purity.

By now a list of boys' names flooded my mind which I passed on to the officer.

I remembered one occasion when Jeff came into his lounge with bundles of gifts and clothes he had bought that day at Heelas in Reading for Peter and Michael. His face lit up with joy as though he were in love. At the time I dismissed it. Realising how much he had missed not being a father, he could snatch the feeling for a short while in his life through other people's children.

I remembered that he would run the boys' bath for

them while they were undressing – because the taps were stiff and the water ran very hot, he said they could have burnt themselves. He would laugh at how the lads openly ran around with nothing on, as they did at home.

He would often rough and tumble with the lads – *all* boys, not just mine. They were about eleven, the age when boys love to test their masculine strength against a man. He would pull them up off the floor by the waistband of their boxer shorts from beneath their jeans. There was one occasion where, for a split second, I felt it getting out of hand and stopped it. It appeared to me as though he was getting a sense of fulfilment from it.

He would tickle the lads and their mates until they were screaming with laughter. He would draw letters on their backs by tickling their skin and they would have to guess the letter he was drawing.

All these things happened in front of people. There was an elderly lady who lodged with them and was almost a family member – she had four children of her own and she never suspected or saw anything.

I told the CPO about the swimming trips from school on a Friday evening and how the boys and their friends would tell how they came down the slide between his legs, as he considered the slides were dangerous for a young lad on his own.

On one occasion I was at Jeff's house and a lad who was now about 28 was staying. Jeff recounted a story of when he had taken this lad, as he was then, swimming with his mates in the holidays. He had gone up to the lad whilst in the pool and kissed him in front of his friends, therefore embarrassing the boy. My eyes popped, but Jeff and the young man were laughing, so although I thought it very odd, the two of them seemed to be OK about it.

I remembered the name of someone who would now be in his late thirties, who had been associated and whose family had been friendly with Jeff for a long time. I did not know how to contact him but I knew roughly where the police could find him. Thinking about it, for some reason I believed he had a story to tell. In January of this year I was sadly proved right.

Jeff was always telling jokes or larking about and teasing children. They loved him for it – he pushed boundaries and said things they would never expect a head teacher to say. He would let the children at school call him 'Uncle Bungle'. Jill, his secretary, would often voice her disapproval. He would sometimes wear a bright wacky wristwatch in preference to his otherwise stylish gold one – because the children commented on it to him.

I remembered how Michael would be violent on some occasions, having spent time with Jeff and without Peter, and how Jeff excused it to me. I remembered the time Heather told me how uncomfortable she felt the day she saw Jeff pull Michael over to him.

I remembered popping round Jeff's Victorian house one Sunday afternoon and notice him taking a blond neighbour's lad upstairs to the bedroom for a maths lesson. At the time, and immediately dismissing the thought, I said, 'Why doesn't he stay downstairs with him? There is the dining room, kitchen, lounge, conservatory, all available and not being occupied by anyone – why isn't he protecting his position?' I immediately shrugged it off as me again being stupid and judgemental. Jeff's style was always different – he used to joke about it to everyone.

I remembered all the video films of Peter and Michael taken on holiday in Padstow. Suddenly, film of them swimming, surfing, coming out of the shower and sleeping in their beds at four in the morning took on a whole new meaning! I wondered if Jeff had ever done anything to Peter and Michael. They had all shared a room. There was a film of the boys running out of the shower, with a towel loosely around them, larking about at bath time as young lads of ten and eleven do.

Now I understood why I was discouraged from going on holiday – *he* wanted time with my boys. I was always told the break from them would be good for me and I was so stressed at the time I never argued the point; because Jeff was right – I was exhausted.

I remembered the day Chris came home with the news that he had passed his A levels in magnificent style – AAB. Jeff was there and gave Chris a big kiss on the cheek. What was all that about?

I remembered the time Roger marched me up to the pub with Eileen after he had heard Michael on the phone to Jeff. I remembered the incident at the new house when Roger decided we were going home and Michael had a £10 note in his hand. I remembered how Roger commented on the way Michael was sat on Jeff's lap.

I remembered once, just before he moved house, going to his bedroom. Roger had banged on so much about his suspicions that for some weird reason I also became momentarily suspicious.

Jeff had a locked filing cabinet in his bedroom, which always puzzled me. I am so ashamed even now to admit to what I did next. I had *never* behaved like this in my whole life and *never* have done since. I went to find the keys and snooped.

Inside I found A to Z filing of neatly documented letters and cards, all of them alphabetically stored according to the boys' names and in pristine condition. I immediately felt this was odd, but *again* I corrected my thoughts. This man was a bachelor about to retire – of course, he would keep memorabilia of his life. He wasn't a dad and wouldn't ever be a granddad; it was perfectly natural to hold these things close to your heart in a sentimental way.

I continued talking to the CPO.

One time my own priest had suggested I become a counsellor. As Jeff had passed his qualifications in counselling, I asked if I might read his notes in order to decide whether I could cope with the course or even for that matter whether I wanted to do so. There was a section where one had to describe sexuality, your own and how you view it and how you recognise it in others. The whole section had been withdrawn from the file. I remember thinking at the time, 'Why would someone hide his or her thoughts about sex?' Jeff had no problem making jokes about sex in the staffroom or anywhere for that matter. However, he was single and could be quite a deeply private and complex person at times.

I remembered Roger telling me, 'Marilyn, the man has passion. He has passion for his religion, music and his teaching. This is not a man with a low sex drive. People with passion definitely have a sex drive, it just isn't directed at women.'

My interview over, I left the room numb and pale. I sat alone in my kitchen, too frightened to visualise what might have happened to my boys. I felt like my whole family and all it stood for had been raped. I felt absolute disgust. I imagined vividly all types of sexual acts of abuse – and wondered whether *my* children had been in the frame. I had no knowledge. However, my mind kept racing. I felt sick and then I was.

Next, it was Roger's turn to share his thoughts on what he had sensed in the short time he had known Jeff.

At some stage, the boys returned home. We were told to bring them into the room. The CPO introduced herself to them and explained who she was. Peter looked stunned and Michael went completely pale.

After Roger, the boys were interviewed. The officer chose to speak to Peter first and then Michael. When Peter came into the kitchen after his interview, he looked ghastly, unable to believe what had just been required of him. He quietly went up to his room to think.

Michael, finally, after twice the length of time Peter was interviewed, came out of the lounge. Like Peter, he was stunned into shock and disbelief. He could hardly speak and had obviously been crying.

I was invited back into the room and the CPO started to reveal her thoughts. She was content that Peter was sexually unharmed, although he was quite naturally shocked regarding the whole situation.

However, she could not decide about Michael. She was certain he was showing classic signs of divided loyalties, and in her mind had definitely been 'seriously groomed'. He displayed a strong desire to keep changing the subject and was shaking and tearful throughout the interview. Being under 18, the police were obliged to tell me their statements.

She told me that, considering they had lived with Jeff, their statements did not relate or match in the same way. Another sign of divided loyalties. I asked how the statements differed.

I had never heard the expression 'groomed' – what did she mean? What was she telling me? I was a teacher – how did I not know or understand about grooming?

She explained that grooming was a tool used by an abuser over many years to worm his way into a person's trust and infiltrate their family. She told me things I had never known.

She explained that Jeff was in fact a nurturing paedophile. This kind can take anything up to ten years working their plan before they strike. I was told Jeff had groomed my ex-husband and I for a long time, using our family stress as a 'way in'.

She explained examples of differing statements. Peter said that Jeff would apparently play games with a bath towel, allowing it to drop so he was then naked. I was horrified! She asked if he wore pyjamas in bed. Peter said no. Michael said yes. When asked to describe the pyjamas, Michael was non-committal and eager to change the subject. She told me of games in the bath. Tickling games. Games can be a cover-up for what is actual abuse. She asked the boys if they thought it odd that at age eleven Jeff helped them at bath time, something their dad and I had not done since they were seven years old. Because it was fun and these were blokes' games, it hadn't occurred to them. Such is the insidiousness of child abuse.

Apparently, the success of the act of abuse lies in the success of the grooming, where touch, nudity, affection, secrecy, trust and a feeling of 'specialness' are established in the victim's mind. The paedophile plays one adult off against the child. Untruths are told about their parents to the child. Eventually, this causes confusion in the mind of the abused, who become unable to face the real issue later on when realisation hits.

It got worse....

With most divorces there reaches a time when everything becomes less than amicable. In our case, it became downright impossible. The realisation hit that, while Jeff was saying less then complimentary things to me about David, he could well have been doing the same regarding me to David! Jeff told me he had no time for David, that even though he was not a father himself, any man could see David was acting irresponsibly. No wonder our tensions were intolerable. Later, the boys confirmed my thoughts had been correct. Jeff had continued to keep meeting up with David, as a friend, having told me he never saw him!

The split was inevitable, but to 'stir the pot' was a cruel act of abuse to us both. David and his new partner met up with us all this year in February. I wanted to show the children, in spite of Jeff's behaviour, that we had solidarity as a whole family. I had always wanted David and I to be friends after the divorce. With four children, there would be many happy occasions to share in the future. It was important for the children, as they forged their own lives and successes that we, as their parents, could enjoy their futures amicably and without atmosphere.

I began to realise that Peter, the twin brother, had been used as the fall guy; he looked Italian – the wrong hair colour and brown eyes. Jeff was always telling me that Peter was made of rubber and was less sensitive than Michael, which I knew at the time was rubbish. They are both sensitive lads, but they manifest it in different ways and styles.

The CPO asked me when I considered the last meeting between Jeff and the boys to have been. I assured her they had not met him since living in West Sussex. I was proved wrong. Apparently, Jeff had remained in contact with David, and on weekends at their father's house he would sometimes arrange to meet up with them somewhere. Before moving here, Roger explained to David the fears he had about Jeff. Like me, David clearly did not believe it either, but continued to maintain contact. Jeff, with David, had sworn the boys to secrecy, never to tell Roger and I. Apparently, Jean had also discussed her fears with David. The CPO had discovered this information from both the boys while questioning them. I was horrified when I found out.

Two cleaners resigned from St Sebastian's School having seen two boys on his lap after school hours. Carney was nuzzling into their necks, and rubbing the insides of their legs. Those boys were my sons! My twin sons! Until today, nobody told me! Why not? Why do people stay silent? All adults have a legal responsibility to protect children and report anything untoward.

My elder son, Chris, then came in from work and he was questioned. He had also been drawn into Jeff's web in the past. Because of Chris's age I was not allowed to know anything from his statement.

Finally, at nine o'clock in the evening, the Child Protection Officer left us to gather up the shattered pieces of our lives and carry on. We were told not to say anything to anyone, as investigations were still ongoing. This instruction was imperative!

I can't find the words, or certainly not enough of them to sum up how I was feeling. Shocked, stunned, sick, violent, horrified, disbelieving, angry, hurt, betrayed, loathing, guilty, dysfunctional, numb. Heartbroken. I thought I would never recover, and I consider myself to be emotionally strong and tough. The depth and breadth of these emotions, changing every minute and lasting 24 hours a day, seven days a week, cannot truly be described. It *has* to be experienced – but it is something, I hope and pray, will never cross your path!

I was no longer allowed for legal reasons to talk to, write to or see Jeff again. I remembered I was supposed to be meeting him at Wisley the following month. I was firmly told to cancel the arrangement, but not in a way that would arouse his suspicions.

I am a useless liar, and I have never tolerated that behaviour in anyone. Roger made contact with Jeff for me on some pretence. However, a couple of times he rang and I had to make excuses that I was in a rush and couldn't talk.

After the CPO left there was a hushed silence and surrealness about the last few hours. From memory, we all went off to our own rooms for some space. Too stunned to talk at length, numb and struggling with our own thoughts and individual pain.

The horror of realising I could possibly have sent my children to a school, every day, which was run by a paedophile would not leave my mind. What parent ever imagines doing that? My best friend could be a paedophile! As a mum, over the years, I had run through my mind perhaps having to face unwanted teenage pregnancies, drugs, alcoholic sons, laziness with school work, storming out after a teenage row – but never, ever this. Who would? Aren't you supposed to meet 'strange men' in parks, after dark, walking alone in woods, fairgrounds and undesirable places? All children attend school – a talented and gifted teacher ran ours, but all was not as it seemed How was I ever going to get my head around this one? How was I ever going to forgive or even understand, or have any understanding? How were my children going to cope?

For the next week every night I would get up at three in the morning and write down the witnessed 'nanoseconds' I had discussed with the CPO. My typed document that went to the police was four pages, on both sides, of A4 paper. The situation filled my mind night and day – every waking and sleeping moment.

In fact, I didn't remember what sleep was, and eventually was given sleeping pills.

I felt awful acting like this – he *had* to be innocent, didn't he?

7

Denial

So maybe Roger had been right all along.

What absolute nonsense!

But then I panicked – what would have happened if Roger and I had never met and the boys had continued seeing Jeff? Somehow, I still couldn't and wouldn't believe it. Everyone was mistaken – this had to be a horrible nightmare and one huge mistake. Roger would say, 'The police haven't come this far and taken eighteen months of research just for the fun of it.' My ears were firmly closed.

Then I became angry with myself – how could I have allowed myself to be taken in by the police? How could I have fallen into the trap of betraying my best friend and allowing my mind to think negatively about the wonderful things Jeff had done? This was my friend...

My friend who had a deep Christian faith for all to see.

My friend who gave everyone his time – particularly the vulnerable.

My friend who had helped form my career as a teacher.

My friend who had taught me so much about teaching.

My friend who showed me the peace of going on retreat at a monastery.

My friend who had brought my children to confirmation.

My friend who understood the anguish of being a mum at times.

My friend who helped look after my children when I was homeless.

My friend who shared the same views of listening and caring for children.

My friend who gave children his time and help when they were confused or finding life hard to handle.

My friend who bought the boys clothes when money was short.

My friend with whom I could talk spiritually.

My friend with whom I could laugh and cry.

My friend who never judged me when I was going through the divorce.

My friend who assured me I was a good mother.

My friend who would invite me to meals with the children so I would eat a decent meal.

My friend who came to see me all those years ago when my baby son was so ill in hospital.

My friend who took my children swimming and to the cinema because I was busy.

My friend who gave my boys holidays because I needed a break.

My friend who I felt privileged to know, honoured that he wanted to be my friend, and a man who I thought was a 'walking saint'.

I have never believed in blind faith in anything or anyone. Jeff had *proved* he was a worthy person whom my family and I could befriend and trust.

But what if the allegations were true? Where did that leave our friendship and everything that had been invested over the years?

No, it couldn't be true. After all, he hadn't admitted

his guilt, if there was any, and was still yet to be arrested. The case had to be passed by the Crown Prosecution Service before any action could be taken.

Jeff was different. Everyone knew he pushed the boundaries. He was never bothered what people thought of him; he felt it was a characteristic of coming from Yorkshire. Calling a spade a spade. He was always challenging the education authorities over bureaucratic attitudes and paperwork. He defended and protected his staff from the rigours of yet another piece of legislation. He encouraged John Redwood MP, the constituent MP at the time, to visit the school. He regularly wrote to the government in support of teachers, and was especially riled by school inspectors, who in his opinion were 'out to unsettle good teachers and make them overly and unnecessarily stressed'.

Yet, when I thought about it, ever since I had known him there had always been a lad or two in his life. They came and went and would stay at his house. This activity was going on when he was a teacher at St Paul's school, Wokingham, before he became head teacher of St Sebastian's. He made a habit of having favourites in school, which the staff noticed. Even the school nurse commented on it. I didn't know what to think and wondered how many boys Jeff may have been grooming. Jeff was a deeply religious, honourable, churchgoing person; he would never have allowed inappropriate behaviour to get in the way of his beliefs – would he?

The police were adamant I was to stay silent. Therefore, I was still unable to discuss the issues banging round my head with any one until his possible arrest. I went round and round the loop repeatedly. I couldn't sleep, eat or function. It continued to take over my thoughts. The whole issue consumed me.

By now, in November 2002, the whole situation, following on from Nicky's accident was too much. I felt I couldn't take any more. Only one thing to do – disappear into a dark hole and never come out. Perfect. If the police were correct and it was true then I was a dysfunctional mother; perhaps I should not have divorced, making a wide-open door, allowing Jeff to walk right through it.

We had been to see Nicky in Durham and we were at a Travel Inn having breakfast. It kept hitting me in waves. I sobbed and sobbed. I could hardly speak. I was a complete wreck and I kept screaming, 'I have held my children's hands and willingly given them into the care of a paedophile – how could I have been so blind? Tell me it is not true!'

How could I have been so dim as not to see something right under my own eyes? I was a teacher, vice-chairperson of governors at the time, a parent and his best friend – how could it have escaped me? I thought myself to be of reasonable intelligence. Hell, I had let down so many people for whom I was responsible whilst wearing all these 'hats'!

I just could not take it in. The tears were splashing over the toast. The waiters and the people sitting at other tables were stunned. It was clear that Roger and I were not having a domestic, but I was distraught. From memory, I think they all did their best to avoid any eye contact.

Silent and strained and unspoken tension was building at home – you could feel it hanging over all of us. We all tried to find other topics to chat and laugh about, in a false attempt to deny the facts.

Then one evening, Chris was in the kitchen and dropped a bottle of ketchup on the floor. From the side profile, Chris and Mike are very similar. I wrongly accused Mike of causing the mess and he completely flipped. He was a sobbing wreck, yelling abuse at me – everything in his mind had suddenly become my fault. We all knew it wasn't my fault, but that was the effect of his grooming. Peter went out of the room to the bathroom to be ill – he could not handle seeing his twin brother in such a state. Chris sat quietly with the two of us, telling us that one day soon he would get his comeuppance – *but when*?!

At some stage, Peter told me Jeff had sat on Peter's bed and asked him if he ever had wet dreams. Peter was only eleven, and hadn't a clue what he was talking about. Therefore, Jeff described it. I was mortified – what other things had been going on I had no idea about? How dare he talk about that without my knowledge or permission? Then I remembered a time when I discovered Jeff had taken one of the boys who was staying with him to the doctor before school. I was furious I did not know there was a problem! Jean, the deputy head has since told me my son apparently had a sore bottom. It just seemed to get worse.

Roger was away working in Birmingham. It broke my heart to see Michael so distressed, and that moment, with every part of me, I truly hated Jeff. If the charge was true, what I wanted to do to him would mean a custodial offence for myself! I had maintained for years that if any person harmed my children, in any way, I would be locked up for my actions. Suddenly, I realised that my children needed me, so I could not put myself in jail. Nevertheless, I wanted to kill him. I truly wanted to kill him.

Michael was very withdrawn and depressed for several weeks and developed psoriasis. I had to tell my mum what was going on at home, as she was picking up that things were not well. What elderly Granny of 78

73

needed to hear this story? It caused her enormous stress. She felt terrible that she hadn't seen the truth and protected her own daughter and grandchildren. The ripple affects were far-reaching, and not just for my family. There had to be other families who had been questioned who were going through the same process.

Late November was the crunch time. I could not live with myself and the possible fact that I may have put my children and others at risk. I bought and stocked up on paracetemol and made a plan of action. Secure in my mind that, for everyone's sake, I was better off dead, I gained calmness and peace.

However, this particular evening we had to go to a dinner party – it was a week before my 50th birthday. I was relaxed and sat next to a lovely neighbour who was a police officer. In confidence, Roger had asked him for some advice a week or so previously. Gareth asked me how I was and I replied I was fine and coping well. I went off to the bathroom and he was waiting in the hall for me before I went back into the dining room. He said, 'He's not worth your spit, you know that, don't you? He isn't worth that much respect to do what you are considering!'

I replied he had no idea what I was considering!

'I do this for a job, I see it every week – how is it going to help anyone?'

Suddenly I realised he could see through me – was I that transparent? *Now* what was I going to do? Gareth would be watching my family.

Anyway, I realised I would be topping myself over an issue which yet had to be proved and could still be a mistake. How could I have been so stupid? Pull yourself together, Marilyn.

When I wasn't in denial, when I allowed thoughts of reality to creep in, then I had horrendous black days contemplating the hideousness of the possible truth. What a totally selfish and irresponsible act suicide would have been. However, the depth of the guilt I felt and not having protected my children, my inability and blindness not to have noticed what was before my eyes, ate away at me like a cancer. The situation totally unbalanced my mind, my emotions and my thinking. It caused a chronic depression and a temporary mental sickness. I found it so hard to live with myself. I was in fact heartbroken.

Christmas came and cards and gifts came from Jeff. I was not allowed to send anything – not that I wanted to do so, knowing what I now knew.

I have always been very strict about thank-you notes. What was I supposed to do with the money he had sent the boys? How could they say thank you? We were not allowed to make contact. The cards had to be handed over to the police.

I knew he would rapidly become suspicious if he did not receive a reply from the boys. Shortly after Christmas Jeff had apparently phoned their dad to find out why he hadn't had a reply, but the boys were not to tell me he was asking!

I phoned the Child Protection Officer in January 2003 to enquire how far they had progressed with proceedings. I was told they had almost gathered the facts and were about to go to Crown Prosecution and then action an arrest with their permission. The person I knew, now in his late thirties, had spoken up and was prepared to give evidence. They had a case.

So I had to tell myself: 'Face the facts, Marilyn – stop denying what appears to be the truth.' But everyone is innocent until proven guilty, aren't they?

Then one morning, I received a call from the CPO, informing me that the CPS had agreed there was a case and they had clearance to arrest Jeff Carney. They did so at about 7 a.m. the next morning. I found out by bumping into a friend from Wokingham at my local Tesco in Horsham! My friend's wife had phoned Jeff that morning, not knowing he was being arrested, and heard the police in the background. Brian, Jeff's friend, briefly told her of the arrest. I can remember walking around Tesco in a trance.

I was shocked – why should I have been? I had lived with this possible scenario since August the year before, but despite approximately six months to prepare myself I realised I wasn't prepared at all.

Jeff was charged and had to report to the police station in three or four weeks.

The phone lines suddenly started melting with activity. A close circle of friends and colleagues who had been forced into such unbearable silence and secrecy were now talking. He had been arrested and there was nothing now to hide.

Could it be true? What did you see? Did you sense anything? Were we overtrusting? It simply can't be true! If it is true, can you imagine the distress it will cause to so many people? Nobody will believe it! Did anyone ever mention anything and not report it? The press would be swarming over this one!

Jeff was a hugely successful and popular, respected head – the school had won a top award for primary schools in Berkshire. Jeff had taught in the county for so many years, this would devastate several hundred people. And what about the church community? This would send them reeling! Jeff had been such a key figure in the church, at times giving the odd sermon on a Sunday.

It amazed me how deep and strong denial can be, how it blocks rational thought. How your mind can't quite push the thoughts into another room. And then there it was – denial over – Jeff returned to the police station at a later date to admit his guilt.

Having admitted his guilt at the magistrates' court, it was therefore true. If only it were that simple. My logical mind was telling me this was true, but, according to the police, I had been groomed for many years and the success of that grooming distorted my thinking and became a barrier to acceptance. Grooming itself is a terrible, destructive act of abuse.

I have always been a crossword fan and I looked up in the thesaurus other words for denial: refute, disclaim, dismiss, repudiate, disavow, rebuff, contradict, negate. Yes, for sure, I had been in denial along with many others.

8

Betrayal

In the New Year, I received a letter from the counsellor at the surgery. My name was now top of the list. I was so relieved, at last, to be able to speak to someone, as I knew the information and talks had to be confidential. What I had forgotten was, I had been referred to her originally because of the fallout from Nicky's accident – poor Sarah had no idea how my life had moved on and the challenge she really faced, and without prior warning!

Before Christmas, our neighbours of three years moved away and a new family arrived. In the first week of January, having only moved in a couple of weeks earlier, Veronica, aged 49, the wife and mother of two, was involved in a fatal car crash on the day of her son's birthday. Her car skidded on ice at a bend and she sadly died a few days after the accident. I felt compelled to help. How do you help someone you hardly know in his or her deepest and darkest hour? I kept thinking, how would I want someone to help me? Would I want space and peace? Would I want a shoulder to cry on? Would I want to go shopping and cook? Would I just want to get drunk to numb everything? This poor family were new to the area, with nobody immediate to turn to. No 'tea bag and tissue' friends.

However awful my problems were, at least nobody I loved had died – although it felt like a large part of my life had been killed, murdered. Struggling with my anger, I felt very fed up with how cruel life had been over a period of almost two years. Would the anguish ever stop? I was determined, however, not to become bitter – that is a destructive path to walk down in every way. You become consumed with self-pity. *That* I was not going to be.

My counsellor helped me sort out all the mixed-up emotion reeling around inside my heart and mind. She helped me come to terms with the fact that my life had changed forever and that realistically I would never 'get over' what had happened. You move on from it a different person, but it is always there ready to bite you in the bum! There are frequent moments when I see someone who resembles Jeff, and I re-enter hell! I attend a children's concert and see youngsters, some of whom will be experiencing abuse, and I re-enter hell. From having been a deeply trusting person, I became overly suspicious of human nature – and I remain less trusting than I ever used to be.

I always thought I knew what anger was, but it hit me that what I had experienced in the past was frustration, exasperation, irritation – not anger. Real anger is pure, it bores through you like a laser, and it was frightening. I was angry at myself, at the people who kept telling me they always knew Jeff was odd and wondered about him – I could have filled the Albert Hall with the number of times I heard that remark. If they were so clever, why did they not say anything at the time? How could I not have thought these things?

Sarah gently helped me peel back the layers of the issue at the base of it all – betrayal. She was right. I had been used and abused, and not for the first time in my life. But all negative emotions link with each other, one fires the other. The more I thought about his actions of betrayal the angrier I became, and the more I considered how my friendship had been betrayed the angrier I became. Occasionally, through an inability to accept the facts as they were, I went around the denial loop again.

When you have been so badly betrayed how do you learn ever to trust again? We decided we would buy a black Labrador puppy. This would teach us to give and receive unconditional love and trust; he would be a distraction and was something the boys had wanted for years. Having a dog would make me leave the house and have to talk to complete strangers again. So in mid-February we all went to Ardingly to collect Max – for the first time in months we all felt real joy and happiness. Max had a job to do – he had to help heal us. We all adored him – and now he approaches his first birthday, he knows he is very special, bless him.

Before Max arrived, I had been spending hours in the garden – the only place where I could find peace. I had spent hours the previous year planning and planting and the effect was clear to see. Now it was February – pruning time. It was a wet and windy day, but I was determined to garden. I was like a demon with a mission. After five hours I had finished. I stepped back to admire my hard work. I had annihilated the garden, I had severely pruned it. There were only stalks left. I even ruined my very sharp loppers!

When Roger and the children came home, they were amazed – where had the garden gone? I explained, 'I think I may have metaphorically and unwittingly removed Jeff's private parts!'

They all burst out laughing, but it was true, and when I told Sarah at the next session, she agreed with me. I then went on to burn the rubbish! I hoped he could feel my actions!

That is what betrayal does – it causes negative and destructive emotions. What is the saying, 'Hell hath no fury like a woman scorned'. How true! 'Don't mess with me' was the message!

Everyone waited for the magistrates' court date. It became clear the huge numbers of people who were suffering badly because of Jeff's betrayal. His secretary, Jill, the boys' godmother, had a terrible time. She could not believe she had defended Jeff – why had she not seen it? How many children had he groomed or even abused whom she felt she should have protected? The staff, who had always been supportive of him, were dreading any interrogation from parents past and present. The school nurse questioned herself repeatedly – how could he be this person?

In my opinion, he had betrayed the Church, the teaching profession, the counselling profession and leaders who work in youth movements, not just friends and families, his own family and staff. He had betrayed the school governors, who trusted and supported him in all he did, believing him to be a honourable person.

Somehow, to my mind, this act of betrayal was as bad as whatever abuse he had committed. He had been such a smooth operator. Had he been someone who did not have the intellect or education to help himself, I would have better understood. He had perpetrated all the grooming and his terrible acts behind a hideous lie, through complete hypocrisy.

As I stated earlier, I have never been able to accept lies. I have always told my children, 'Whatever you have done, tell me the truth. If you lie, the effect of that will be far worse for you than what you have actually done.'

My mum always said, 'I would rather know a thief than a liar.' My dad would quote, 'Be honest and upstanding, representing what is good and true.'

It is the deception, unfaithfulness, disloyalty, double-crossing and duplicity that hurts so much.

We are all victims of our upbringing. In my case, I was educated at a convent school in Southampton, where honesty and integrity mattered. My parents put a high value on these qualities, and on being accountable and responsible for the way you live your life and the message it gives others. Many things I may be, but I know I have integrity and honesty.

What Jeff had done went completely against my core beliefs, both spiritual and secular. I felt deeply for all the other people who were now talking about the case and who were having difficulty with it. I felt so sorry for his sister, who is a lovely lady. I phoned her putting her mind at rest that nobody believed she knew anything. She was experiencing the same emotional cocktail; in her case, he was her brother, so it was much harder for her to take the position of walking away – they had always been very close and supported each other. I really felt for her and her family, because they loved him, and although they could not condone his actions they had to be there for him.

I told people that I would have felt less betrayed than this if I'd discovered my husband had been having an affair. At least an affair with another woman would be normal. Many were amazed at my thoughts and feelings, but that is how it felt.

What had my children done to be so badly betrayed? They were innocent victims. They felt so used and manipulated, which they had been. They had invested their emotions, time and energy in this friendship. They were only 16. Chris, my eldest son, was 22. Was there anything he missed which he perhaps wished he had spoken about at the time, which could have protected us from further harm? What a burden to have to carry at his age. None of it his or my blame or responsibility.

As we all slowly went down a dark pit of depression, Roger kept telling us, 'It is not your weakness to blame here at all – it just shows the strength of his manipulation.' Jeff was a practised master at it.

That phrase ran through my brain many times a day to keep me sane, and I repeated it to others who were struggling. Sarah had to keep reminding me repeatedly that this was not my guilt. I now regularly visited Alton Abbey and my friend Father William was giving me the same message. Having been a regular churchgoer all my life, I could no longer attend conventional church for fear of being betrayed by another impostor. We all have our dark and less attractive side to be sure, but we don't all break the law and deceive to this extent. I could not bring myself to sit through a service where I had to listen to a sermon, shake hands and 'share the peace' with the person sat behind and next to me – just in case...

Jeff would, at times, preach on a Sunday, so I refused to sit and listen to another human being telling me from the pulpit how I should live my life, only to find they might be even more flawed than I. At 50, I know the rules and how to put it right if I go wrong. I preferred to practise my faith quietly and reflectively at the abbey – the betrayal meant I could not trust as I once had. Jeff had no right to change the way I lived my life alongside others, but in order not to be so deeply and painfully deceived again, I had to change. I daren't risk being hurt this way again, even with different reasons behind the betrayal. I would not survive a second time – I was already struggling to do so.

Jeff clearly targeted the way I admired people who didn't conform, the eccentric, and the fact that I have always tried to be non-judgemental and non-prejudiced. All this was now being challenged. Was I really the person I hoped I was? I fought with not becoming bitter and twisted; I had to find other ways to transform all the negativity into a positive situation.

I was still on a variety of tablets and still unable to return to work. It was difficult to find an outlet. I was unable to face everyday problems. I became incapable of speaking to the bank. Bills went unpaid. I could not work. Roger stayed at home some days to be with me; he lost contracts and business, and therefore income, as a result.

One day I was driving past Sotheby's which is on the approach road to Billingshurst. There was an enormous banner advertising St Catherine's Hospice, with an email address. It was there the next day as well. I decided if it was still there on day three then it was meant for me, and sure enough, there it was. I stopped the car and came home, emailed the management and went to see them.

I thought, 'Well, no one in my family has died, things *could* be worse.' Maybe, if I volunteer to help at the hospice, I will gain by being with people far worse than my family or I. I still work there now, and I love the atmosphere of genuine warmth, humour and tangible love for everyone within the building – staff, patients and visitors – all there for a mutual purpose, everyone attempting to make a difference. It took me out of myself, and slowly I could feel my strength returning. I was beginning to heal. I could feel positive again.

9

Empowered to Fight Back – the Campaign

On 8th April 2003 at the magistrates' court, the case was referred to the Crown Court. Jeff admitted his abuse of two young boys with a 20-year gap – which meant it was an historic case with the legal people. The magistrate said Jeff had committed a terrible act of betrayal, worming his way into a family's affections, then going on to abuse the sons of friends.

The police disallowed Jeff from having any further contact with people who they had interviewed – to do so would have meant his immediate arrest. What a relief!

I did not know at that time who the second boy was. I noticed the date of the offence – I was horrified. It was the same year as the last New Year's Eve dinner I went to at Jeff's. Once again, the anger returned. What if the mum, whoever she was, thought it OK to send her son to stay at Jeff's because I was always around? What would she think of me? Would she think I was condoning his behaviour and covering for him? Who was she? Who was he? How could I explain that I knew and saw nothing?

I found myself imagining over and again the most revolting scenarios, which may have happened. I wondered, did he masturbate these lads? Did they have to masturbate him? I also wondered whether he performed oral sex, with them reciprocating. I needed to find out the legal difference between molesting, indecent assault, gross indecency, buggery and the like, for my own personal understanding.

By May, my doctor insisted Roger should take me away from it all. We went to Ravello in Italy. We walked, slept for hours at a time, read, talked and sat in bars watching the world go by. I bought copious amounts of leather goods in Sorrento. On my return, however, Max the wayward puppy chewed every pair of Italian shoes I had purchased!

The day after we returned from Italy, my sister rang to say Mum had fallen in Southampton city centre. She had broken her hip and needed a replacement. Whilst awaiting the court case, my sister and I and our families were thrown into having to rehouse Mum, as it was impossible and impractical for her to return to the home she had spent 50 years of her life in; the home where we all grew up and, in fact, where I was born. She finally moved to her brand-new flat mid-July.

Eventually, 17th June 2003 arrived – the date of the trial at Reading Crown Court, with Judge Stanley Spence presiding. It felt as though we had waited a lifetime for this date. I had toyed with the idea of being at the court. This idea was immediately swept aside by my doctor and counsellor. They were concerned that I was only just 'coming back', and should the case go pear-shaped it would have an adverse effect on my health. So I stayed at home, eagerly awaiting the result. I was jumpy from the moment I awoke, trying to imagine the court and how Jeff must be feeling – surely he must feel so ashamed of himself.

During the afternoon the phone rang, and I could

not believe my ears. Jeff had received £150 costs, a community rehabilitation order for three years, and was required to attend a sex offenders' programme. He was also told not to sleep under the same roof as a 16-year-old for the next three years. I was incensed – numbed. I felt shocked, angry, and let down by the justice system. Did the judge have no idea about child abuse, or rather family abuse, and all it entails? What was wrong with the judge? What was he thinking of? This man was in a trusted and respected position! What message did the judge's decision send out to other offenders and to victims?

Two victims came forward, but it didn't mean there were not more! Most children, especially boys, find it amazingly difficult and humiliating to speak about this crime done to them, and would therefore choose to stay quiet. And the judge had not issued an order disallowing his contact with children. Children were still at risk!

I was concerned. The criminal-record checks prove nothing other than the fact you have been caught. However, some schools, even now, do not always instigate those checks. My own check was done in West Sussex two years ago. A certificate that Mrs Marilyn *Haines* had a clear record was issued to me. Excellent, Mrs Haines didn't *exist*. I rang the bureau, who were anxious I return the certificate (which I did, though I kept a copy of their error!). I pointed out how happy I would be if I were a paedophile, and how easy it is to slip through the net. I then wondered if plumbers, electricians and other contractors who enter schools have criminal checks done? If not, why not? I still have not had an answer.

Jeff needed a restriction order on him, and the judge should have given that. I was told that the judge went on to say he could 'make the exceptional decision in this case to issue a non-custodial sentence because of the man's remarkable references and good character'. And what difference exactly did that make? Since when did being a nice person of 'good character' mean you were exempt from the law?

I was furious and immediately rang the Child Protection Unit at Thames Valley Police. They were similarly horrified. The ex-chair of governors had stood in the witness box as a character witness supporting Jeff's honourable character and testifying that he had given the school '17 golden years'. This infuriated me; he could have gone to the court as a friend, but I was vice-chair at the time when he was chairman – he didn't ask me what I thought. He certainly had no remit to speak for the school. My children were numb with shock. We felt sick and let down. Robbed of any justice.

Another issue emerged – a robed abbot from an abbey where Jeff regularly went was in court. How could the Church be seen to take a position of such obvious support outside of the monastery? He was in court alongside the victims. What about the support for them? What message was he giving about the Church?

I had to do something – but what? I couldn't live with myself just to leave it hanging there – it all felt so wrong. I could not, and would not calm down. Something had to be done. Roger and the boys came home from work and school in total disbelief. They stood shaking their heads.

We had already read in the papers, following the magistrates' court appearance, about how he abused these lads. At that time, I realised I had personally witnessed, along with others, his tickling games and romping and wondered whether I had actually been watching his abuse. It made me feel sick. How could the judge think he was a nice man? Surely, his good character was on the line? He lacked integrity. I wondered whether his good character and good work were merely a manipulative cover to distract from the darker side he hid so well.

On the same day at the Old Bailey, a man was sentenced to 12 months in jail having downloaded 200 pictures of child porn from the Internet. Although inappropriate, he had not at that stage actually harmed anyone. Where was the consistency of justice? Judge Stanley Spence had shown no continuity with the opinion of the magistrates' court. How could Jeff have ended up with a lesser sentence than that recommended by the previous court?

I rang the Child Protection Officer again, and hounded her to take the matter up with the Crown Prosecution Service. I was told it was impossible – I could shout and rant for all my worth, but there was nothing I could effectively do to change the decision!

I became quite assertive saying, 'Is that so? The CPS must have a boss. They surely don't have such a protected position they can never be challenged. I am sorry but I refuse to accept what you are telling me!'

That was the moment I began my strategy. I knew about human rights, but it was about time it went down on the side of the victims and their families. When you violate someone else's rights in this way, to my mind you have invalidated any right to your own!

I checked with my family – was it OK with them if I campaigned for a change in the decision? I absolutely confirmed, if at any time it was too much for any one of them, I would stop. I was doing it for them as well as for the victims, their families and friends, myself and my ex-colleagues.

I went back to Alton Abbey and I discussed with Father William whether I should take matters further with the courts. Was I being vindictive and malicious? Was it spiritually the correct action to take? William explained that there is righteous anger. Although I was in no way responsible for Jeff's actions, I did have a responsibility to act for the benefit of others, and would be sent the strength to cope.

Father William explained that abuse is about power. The abuse, inappropriately and wrongly, makes the abused feel awkward, distorted, embarrassed, sensitive and silent! The abused *must* claim back the power taken from them, put a stake in the ground, face the abuser and become empowered to fight back. He explained that unless this happens, the manipulator still has the control and the pull of the strings, even if they live in another area. The strength of the manipulation continues in the mind unless it is conquered.

So I fought!

The police appreciated what I was attempting to do. However, they felt there was nothing I could affectively achieve. Judges cannot be questioned or challenged.

I have always tried to follow this prayer and have always found it helpful to sort out my mind: 'Grant me the serenity to accept the things I cannot change, the courage to change the things I can, and the wisdom to know the difference.' I still had not found serenity – but I was certainly going to find the courage, in the hope it would result in my serenity.

Throughout all of this, and Nicky's accident, I have never lost my faith. Religion is something different! Created by man, corrupted by man for man's use and abuse, in my opinion! My faith remains stronger than ever. I truly believe in a God, His Son and the Holy Spirit. How do I know? Because I have experienced it

– particularly the empowerment of the Holy Spirit? Personally, I do not believe in coincidence or luck; for me it is all preordained. You bump into someone one day – you were meant to meet. You achieve the impossible – you have been empowered. I would stress I am not religious, but spiritual – they are not the same thing.

I sat quietly and, yes, prayed that if I challenged the decision I might well put someone behind bars. Was it really the right thing to do? I went back again to Alton Abbey to see Father William; he gave it his blessing. These things are important to me; one day I will have to answer for how I lived my life and why I acted in certain ways – I had to have guidance that I was on the right track for the right reasons.

I passionately believe in the rights of a child to have a loving and stable environment, free from the torment of adult behaviour. I realise I live in an idealistic frame of mind, but, I reasoned with myself, if nobody ever puts a stake in the ground, nothing will change. 'Do what you always did and you will get what you always got.'

I *had* to attempt to force a change. What did I have to lose? I was no longer teaching, and therefore was not tied into a contract of loyalty to the system. I was no longer a governor, and I had moved away – I could discreetly carry out a campaign. Being a mother, teacher, governor and churchgoer – or I should say, Christian – I wanted to defend so many corners for myself, and for others.

I discovered the elder victim, having had the courage to give the police a case, had hit a 'low', which concerned them, after he heard about the Crown Court decision. I felt I owed it to him – after all, I had given the police the clue, and this brave man had delivered

93

the necessary information to form a case, when he could have chosen to walk away. He assisted in bringing the truth into the open and needed, even deserved, righteous support. He did it for the protection and support of other children – an action to be admired.

I had challenged the courts before when I needed to be rehoused after my divorce – I could do it again! I had won on that occasion – why shouldn't I be successful once again? How would I know unless I tried? I didn't accept NO then, I wasn't going to do so now either!

So, armed with the knowledge that I would never succeed, I began writing my letters. It hurt to do so. Pulling against my anger was deep sadness. This man had been so close to me and, seemingly, at the time had done so much to support me, and now I felt I was destroying him. I questioned myself repeatedly. It came down to one thing – I never really knew the man at all. He had severely broken the law and children's lives – not run off with the day's takings! It had to be done before he harmed any other child, friend or family.

I sat for hours day and night on the computer. I would get up at about four in the morning for about four weeks and type furiously as I thought of the next person to write to. I spent hours on the phone explaining my case to people and checking the correct names of those to whom I should send documents.

Everyone I wrote to received everybody's letters. I sent them by special delivery; there could be no argument about their receipt – there would be a signature if anyone denied it. I kept everyone in the loop.

I asked St Sebastian's Church if there was anything on record about Jeff. Lo and behold, he had written an article in the church magazine where he described himself and his holiness! In this article he stated, 'I feel I can thank God for His guidance in everything. Regrets? I have none, other than the times I have consciously or unconsciously hurt others. I can, however, rely on God forgiving me. Whilst training as a monk I learnt we should not blame other people for problems with relationships, and come to a fuller realisation of "self". The vow of obedience was difficult, as I had always wanted to challenge the authority of people above me, perhaps one of the most important qualities of leadership. My experience as a Franciscan was good and I was able to see what I really was. We were not able to pretend. You are what you are but God loves you just the same.'

I sent this article with every letter, to help people understand how we had been deceived.

What hypocrisy! Now we know the truth! Having read the Gospel of Matthew, chapter 18, verses 3 to 12, I now wonder what Jeff feels his fate might be in the next life. Here is an extract from verses 6 and 7:

But whoso shall offend one of these little ones which believe in me, it were better for him that a millstone were hanged about his neck, and that he were drowned in the depth of the sea.

Woe unto the world because of offences! For it must needs that offences come: But woe to that man by whom the offence cometh!

Chilling stuff for us all!

I began to gather any newspaper articles regarding Jeff and any other paedophile case where there had in my opinion been weak sentencing, and sent them with the letters. I went to see Francis Maude, my constituency MP. Roger and I spent about 45 minutes with him at his surgery. I admit to becoming emotional. I urged him to think how he would feel if this were his daughters. The doorbell rings, the police are there, they explain why and your life is changed forever. He promised me he would personally speak to John Redwood and the Attorney General. I wrote to John Redwood, constituency MP for the school where Jeff was head teacher.

I wrote to children's support organisations – Childline, NSPCC and Kidscape. I spent two hours with Bishop Lindsay of Horsham – I was incensed that a robed abbot had been in court to support a self-admitted abuser. I wrote to the Abbot who appeared in court, asking him why he had been there – would he not have been more effective praying for Jeff in chapel? What message had it given the victims about the loyalties of the Church? This person had killed someone's trust, stolen his innocence, coveted something which was not his to have, and hardly loved another as himself!

I wrote back to the C of E Child Protection Unit, after they had written to me requesting I should not be negative about the court decision. I suggested, if that was their position, then perhaps they might have more information than I about anything positive regarding child abuse. To this day, I have not received a reply!

Letters also went to the CPS, Tony Blair, Iain Duncan Smith, Harriet Harman QC, the *Church of England Newspaper* and other newspapers. I wrote to the *Reading Evening Post* explaining that once again our courts appeared to have made another faux pas with ineffective and weak sentencing.

I wrote to, emailed or phoned all the major newspapers and TV programmes such as *Richard and Judy*, *BBC Breakfast* and so on. Amazingly most replied and asked me to keep them updated! I was building quite a network of contacts!

This is how the campaign unfolded. I looked back after every letter I wrote; they were from the heart – I couldn't believe I had written them. I don't believe I could right the same letters again. I was sent the energy and drive, I was a foot soldier, if you choose to see it that way. Well, that is my belief. For me, my faith the only thing that stays constant, undistorted. It never abandons me; it is reliably there!

Finally, I wrote to the Attorney General. I had written to everyone except the Queen!

I would wait ten days for a reply from people – if I did not receive one, I would back it up with phone calls and further letters.

All this activity took place day and night over four weeks; it cost £300 in stationery, photocopying and postage. My file of letters is two inches thick. I suppose I must have written 30 to 40 letters, but it was worth it. There is *nothing* in my life I can say I have felt with such conviction and passion – I knew I was acting for the best, and right reasons. A greater force was driving me on.

The cashiers in the village post office were very interested in how my strategy was developing. They gave me discounts to help towards the cost, to show their support.

I suppose, with hindsight it became my *raison d'être*. It obsessed my every waking and sleeping hour. Hideous for my family, although they supported me. I was NOT going to go away or roll over and die, or take NO for an answer. I believed in my mission *that* much. It mattered – for everyone's sake. Friends and family became very concerned as all this activity was exhausting me and I wasn't sleeping or eating. I was also constantly worried about how Peter and Michael really were. My fears for them never left me – they were right in the middle of their AS levels and needed all this like a hole in the head. However, they wanted me to continue – so I did. My feelings of guilt over it all would frequently creep in.

I received dozens of letters arriving in special envelopes. Remarkably, the postman had begun to call out and wave to me – I realised he must have thought I was an important member of state, with all the obvious postmarks on the mail I was receiving!

In late July, the magical moment arrived. The Attorney General, the Rt Hon Lord Goldsmith, had written to confirm that he was reviewing the case through the Court of Appeal because of unduly lenient sentencing. I thought I had won the lottery. I could have kissed him. All my efforts, my ranting and the innumerable visits to the local post office had paid off.

Who was it who said I could never achieve it? I rang Child Protection and informed them that they owed me a drink in the local! I screamed and shrieked – the children thought the dog had been taken ill!

Although I was amazed, in my heart I knew I would win – I was the only one who never doubted it. If necessary, I would have chained myself to the Houses of Parliament, I believed in the cause that much. At no time did I intend to disappear, or take NO for an answer. Therefore, we waited for the Court of Appeal date, which we were told would be within three months of the referral. We looked forward to October!

During this time I had made contact with Jo Evans, who is now my business partner and friend! She had been abused by her headmaster while a child, and had taken him to court two or three years previously and has since written a book. She advised me to take a break and to stay quiet and relax through the summer, as when October came the activity would be tremendous and exhausting to handle in every way. She was right!

Not having heard by late September, I rang the Attorney General's office and was told that the case would be in the next week. I was sat with Jo at the time. We had only a week to go!

The nerves were jangling. We prepared for the date, and I frenetically rang the press, TV and radio. I wanted as much publicity as possible to support the cause – why go quietly? Everyone I had contacted in June and July remembered me, and all were happy to support with media activity on the day.

The afternoon before the date, we heard from the Child Protection team that the case had been deferred for two weeks! The let-down, and the waiting, was horrendous. None of us had slept properly, and now we had to elongate the agony. We couldn't sit down. I had so many calls to make to stop the press going to print the following morning!

I worried in case there was a problem. I was told that the judges had chosen to sit for two days and listen to a group of similar appeals, rather than hear them all separately on different days.

We now had to wait until Friday 17th October 2003. The countdown started all over again. The two weeks felt like forever to begin with, but we carried on as if life was normal for us and it went quicker. I think we were all carrying our secret thoughts and tensions around with us day and night. Conversation remained around whose football team had bought which players for the coming season, and the cricket results.

I then realised I had no idea what to wear. My counsellor was preparing me for microphones in my face – what was I going to say? Anything? Nothing? Was I going to continue to campaign generally for a real change in the law? Had I thought about it? It hit me – what had I started? No stopping it now!

My good friend Lynn was brought in to discuss wardrobe colours. Not red or pink in case I got hot and flushed. Nothing too official-looking or too mumsy. Smart and elegant we settled for. Fortunately, during this time of waiting I had become something of a shopaholic. I had actually told Lynn I couldn't stop buying from Next – I had acquired six pairs of boots and endless suedette skirts and assorted tops. Then there was the fortune I was daily spending in Tesco on all types of extravagant food for the children. I felt guilty about spending the money, but I couldn't stop!

Lynn decided on a beige and olive-green ensemble, my new mink-suede boots and matching bag. I borrowed one of her scarves. She chose a tawny lipstick with matching nail varnish to be painted the night before.

I hardly slept that night; we had to be up so early – 5.15 a.m., to be exact. I was terrified we would oversleep and miss the train.

The morning arrived and Roger, the twins and I left the house at six-thirty in the morning for the early train. Nobody spoke. The boys were shattered and looked more like offenders than attendees! We all slept on the train on and off, and casually read the papers.

We arrived at the courts and went into a cafe opposite for croissants and coffee. Again nobody spoke. Suddenly my phone rang – it was Meridian TV. The fun and games was starting!

The four of us looked open-mouthed at each other in amazement. I suddenly felt very sick and nervous. We could not believe the media and press interest. Sky TV, BBC, ITN and all the national papers. A barrister arriving for work stopped and asked me if I was anyone famous! I replied, 'Not at all – it is just another paedophile appeal case!' And he wished me luck.

I knew this was it. After today, there was nothing more I could do legally, which is why I backed up with media and press to get the widest exposure possible. The law of this land *had* to change.

10

The Day of Reckoning

We waited outside Court 8 to be greeted by Harriet
Harman QC. I was very impressed with the courtesy
and respect given to us by all the officials. She explained
the procedures, and the Attorney General's office staff
had provided a child protection officer, even though
our own were attending, and a Crown Prosecution
adviser. The prosecution counsel introduced themselves
and once again took us through the procedures.

Because Jeff was not in custody, he chose not to be
there. I was disappointed, as I would have loved to
stare at him to see if he would dare to make eye
contact. My counsellor and Father William had prepared
me; if he was there I was to smile and walk on with
my head held high.

'The court will rise!' This was it! My heart was
pounding as we sat through six other gruelling accounts
of similar behaviour before Jeff Carney's case was
called. Lord Justice Kay and his colleagues were clearly
doing their best to understand the plight of the victims.

One comment was made: 'If an abuser shows remorse,
it is a free country – why wait until you are arrested!'
Good point – one that I had already pointed out in my
letters. If Carney was remorseful, why had he not
written to anyone? I was always taught, as a child,

true remorse is having the courage to say to those whom you have hurt, 'Please can you find it in your heart to forgive me!'

Carney's defence counsel pointed out the excellent character references he had received. Lord Justice Kay commented that he didn't think we were questioning his honesty, although perhaps we were. Did the defence not realise the dreadful things Carney had done? How could any right-minded person give a character reference – unless they were unaware of the facts of the crime? Lord Justice Kay could see the confusion in the victim's mind affecting his childhood.

I could not take my eyes off the panel of judges. The debate went on. I struggled to concentrate. I dared not hope – was I hearing correctly? Had I imagined Carney's defence counsel was being given a 'grilling'?

We were then told that because there were so many cases the final judgement and summing up would be the following Thursday – 23rd October. Another wait! Another week of intolerable tension, and, oh no, another outfit needed!

We came out of the court and the CPS asked how we felt; they felt 'pleased' with the way the case went. This was interpreted by the other officials and the press as 'Basically, Marilyn, they believe he will be sentenced – relax!'

We all went off to the pub, and finally rolled onto the train back home several hours later! We all fell asleep. As we walked home, Peter and Michael stopped and gave me an enormous hug, saying, 'Well done, Mum, and thank you.' I burst into tears.

I was straight on the phone to Lynn the following day for another costume discussion. This time she settled on all black, giving another pair of new suede boots and bag an airing! She loaned me a pale jacket she had bought six years previously, and another scarf. I found a black suede belt from years ago at the base of a drawer. This time I was to wear red lipstick and matching varnish. We stepped back, pleased with the effect, and waited.

Life at home continued in the same state of pretence – going through the motions of normal living whilst carrying this huge stress. I must have done the ironing and housework, walked the dog, met friends. I don't remember any of it, apart from the fact that I was still shopping for Britain – amazing as in reality I hate shopping and do anything to avoid it.

Thursday 23rd October meant another early start. The poor boys had not realised that there was an hour before six in the morning – they had now experienced the like twice within a week.

Once again we sat in silence on the train, possibly even more nervous than before. This time the press and media presence was even greater! The lads were amazed, and quite excited that their mum was going to be in the papers and on TV. There were interviews and photo shoots before we went into court, with promises obtained that we would be available after the judgement.

'The court will rise.' Here we go again – for the last time. Would my efforts have paid off? Had I done enough? It was too late now.

We sat through half an hour of legal jargon. Having once thought I might like to have been a barrister, I was now very pleased I had chosen teaching. So many reference books. So much data to remember.

Lord Justice Kay explained that the panel had overturned all cases except one. Naturally, I thought, 'OK – shall we go now? Surely he can't have escaped again!'

Two cases before Jeff's had not been overturned,

but toughened. The reality was slowly sinking in – he was going to be sentenced! I held tight to Peter and Michael's hand and shut my eyes. The court said that it overturned the previous judgement to a custodial sentence of 15 months – 5 months for each assault. Given double jeopardy discount, what should have been 30 months is now 15 months. The court said that a restriction from working with children will run for 10 years, and that Carney must report by 12 noon the next day at Basingstoke Police Station.

I could *not* stop shaking, the tears spilled over. I looked up to the sky and said, 'Thank you, God!' My legs had turned to jelly and I could not move. Within five minutes, the judgement of all cases was over and the judges had left. I could have kissed them!

The courtroom emptied. I still could not stand, I still shook from head to foot. I practised the deep breathing from my labour-ward days; slowly I re-entered Earth! Roger urged me to take my time and gather my senses before leaving the court – he already had an idea of the media presence waiting outside the doors.

He was right. Immediately outside the court doors were *so* many print journalists, and radio and TV reporters. It was surreal – why were they so strongly interested? I made a general statement of how I felt and any other opinion, and was then ushered outside for Sky Live TV, ITN and BBC.

I walked down the steps outside into the sunshine. Peter held my arm. 'Well done, Mum – how does it feel?'

'Pete, I have just helped someone to go to jail – how horrible am I?'

'Mum, he has put himself in jail and should have been there since June for two and a half years. Had the original judge done his job correctly... Forget him, Mum – we are all so proud of what you have done.'

Michael was gobsmacked. 'Oh, my God, Mum – have you seen all the camera crews? Am I walking in someone else's life? This is what other people do.'

I had to agree with him – the feeling was very surreal. At this time of day, I would normally be walking the dog through the fields, meeting a friend for lunch, shopping. Here I was being chased around by reporters. I remember not being at all concerned about what I would say – I had rehearsed it a hundred times. I was more worried that I might have lipstick on my teeth!

Suddenly, I found myself saying to the media that I would continue campaigning for zero tolerance and a change in the law. What was I saying? Was that true? Yes, why not? It seemed pointless, having put in all this effort and interest, for it to be wasted. Apparently, my counsellor was watching and said, 'Oh, my God, I knew she would carry on!'

I did close to 20 interviews that morning and early afternoon. We were treated to so many congratulatory drinks in the bar by press and barristers. The boys loved it and at one time Michael was arguing football tactics with a leading barrister like they were old mates! We rushed off to see Sky again, then to the ITN and BBC studios. The lads could not believe how TV presenters appear to be sitting in luxury, when in reality a couple of chairs, a lamp and a plant are stuck in a corridor by the toilets and coffee machine, and filming starts! They were constantly texting their friends with the next media update. We were in the pub when the news came through to the media – 'Gordon Brown's wife has had her baby.' The lads were thrilled to know before the rest of the nation!

I was overawed by the attention. Why were they so interested in me? Paedophile cases seem to be in the papers almost every day. A couple of journalists explained: 'You have made history, that's why!'

'How?'

'You are the first person to reach the Court of Appeal simply by your own efforts and strategy and letter writing, and without petitions or lawyers. Secondly, you are the first person to so so who is not a direct relative of the victim witnesses – well done!'

It didn't sink in at first – all I ever wanted and worked for was to help the victims feel better about things, ensure Jeff was kept away from children, and that all his one-time supporters knew the truth about the man, which hopefully in time would help them to overcome their denial.

Back we went to the pub for celebratory drinks, which were being bought for us, and the largest steaks you can imagine. I think it was the first time in two weeks I had noticed the taste of food!

The boys had learnt so much about life over the two days. I have often said, even though I am a teacher, that not all the best education is in class!

Finally, we caught the train home, yet again the worse for wear, but, nevertheless, very happy. I spent the whole time phoning friends and family. The lads were still texting their friends back and forth, as my face was appearing everywhere. The secret was over. Our lives could begin to move on.

On arriving home, there were 15 messages on the phone from TV, radio, magazines and newspapers. We were still receiving calls at one in the morning.

The following day, the phones didn't stop. Roger and I were talking from seven in the morning to seven at night, when we switched the phones off for our own sanity. Every time we finished a call, it would ring back 'You have three new messages.'

On the Saturday, we were up at four in the morning to drive to London for the BBC Radio Five Live show – I was being interviewed at seven in the morning. From there, we went on to LBC studios for a half-hour interview broadcasting at eight o'clock in the morning, and finally on to meet Sara Payne for a couple of hours, and a photo shoot for the *News of the World* to support the For Sarah campaign. What a remarkable woman Sara is, and also her children. I also wrote the supporting article for the *News of the World* printed that Sunday.

We were exhausted and yet elated. From memory, we crawled into bed at eight in the evening that night and slept for 12 hours! From the moment I walked from the court, my life changed in more than one sense – and so did Jeff's.

11

What about Roger and the Children?

A couple of weeks before the case was heard, Michael had an outburst which upset me badly. It was obvious that he, like the rest of us, was becoming tense about the outcome.

I had taken enough of being someone's verbal punchbag – brought about by Jeff – and I was near the end of my rope. I was still seeing my counsellor every two weeks, and she was becoming concerned that I was pushing myself to the limit. That night I felt I had reached it!

The following evening Michael asked Roger if he could go out for a drink with him for a chat. Roger looked at me and said, 'I think Michael is about to say things he has never said before – with any luck and it will release him.'

My worst suspicions were true, but I was thankful I now knew. The boys were encouraged to write down how they saw things, and how they were used. The written word is cathartic – which is the reason I have written this book! I would recommend it to anyone.

With the lads' permission, I have included their own accounts. They want to help other children and families, if they can, from falling into the same trap. Roger and I, and their school, are immensely proud of the way they have coped. My Dad used to say, 'If it doesn't kill you, it can only make you stronger.' I applaud them.

Michael's document: Michael is 17 years old at the time of writing this.

Jeff Carney

Jeff Carney was the head teacher where my brothers, sister and I all went. Jeff had been a family friend since my eldest brother had started and became closer when my twin brother and I were born. My first memories of Jeff are on my first days when I started at school. He was the headmaster.

There were occasions when he would take the class for gym practice. If people were to achieve something good during these sessions he would give away chocolates, which he kept in his office. In assemblies once a week he would always tell jokes or play silly little games and I found him more enjoyable to be around than any other teacher.

By the time I got to Year 5, aged about 9–10, I found that living at home was getting harder and harder as my mum and dad were always fighting and arguing. Jeff knew what was happening at home because my mum had been a teacher in the school and remained friends after she left. The first time I visited his house was when my mum went around to talk about work and we all went.

It is during this time that my relationship with Jeff grew. When I got to know him a bit better, and I could see that my mum and dad both thought highly of him I did too. There were times I would sit in his office, crying, and tell him what I felt about the situation at home and about how fed up I was. He kept telling me everything was going to be OK because God looks after everyone and he was praying for our family.

Visits to his house became more frequent, especially when my mum and dad's relationship got to the worst stages. These visits turned into visits where Jeff would look after my brother and me and they eventually turned into overnight visits. He would often take us out for the day, occasionally to London to visit places such as the Tower of London, Tower Bridge, etc. I considered him to be my best friend. There then came a time that he was planning a holiday down in Cornwall in which he asked whether me and my brother would like to go with him, which we did.

When my mum and dad were getting a divorce, we had sold the house without having found a new one. My mum, brother and sister all lived with a friend and my twin brother and I went to live with him and he became our guardian. This arrangement stayed like this for a few months until my mum had found a new house. Mum would come and visit as often as she could and my dad would only come occasionally, which my mum didn't know about.

Jeff would always make me feel the favourite and more special than any of my brothers and sister, which I enjoyed because I have never had that much attention before or since from a carer/guardian. After we moved into our new house, I continued to see him and stay for a day, weekends, etc. Things that happened at his house only happened there and back at home things were different, I just felt that it was the way it was. I remember him always telling me that he was more concerned about me than my brother because I was falling out with my mum quite often. He said that he always believed that one day I would fall out so badly that I would run away from home. I never questioned this, I just accepted and believed that one day it would come true. I was regularly arguing with my mum, but never ran away. When mum first met my current stepdad, he never seemed to appreciate Jeff and always thought that he would never marry my mother.

Although I was obviously being 'groomed' and 'abused', it never felt like that, as everything was always made fun. The only time I had ever thought it was odd to have a friend like him was describing him to a friend when I was in Year 8, aged 12. I remember clearly thinking that why did no one else have a friend like Jeff but I did? However, I dismissed this thought and believed that it was a unique relationship in what had been awkward circumstances when mum and dad were getting divorced.

The day I came home from school/college to find the police at my house wanting to interview me, it came as a complete shock as I had always dismissed any queries I had about Jeff. I was extremely confused because I couldn't understand why a man who had always appeared to be kind, generous and fun could do the things that he had done. The hardest thing for me to get over was that I couldn't understand why people who said they weren't surprised when they found out didn't say anything at the time and allowed this man to continue in his everyday life putting every boy pupil at the school in danger. Then every bad emotion possible went through me as I was told that this man had abused his power of authority, manipulated people and abused children and then got away with a non-custodial sentence. I found myself questioning the justice system, because it was crystal clear to me that justice had not happened. I had always believed a lack of justice on this scale was not possible in our country. But, the case eventually went to the Court of Appeal, which was great news. As I sat in the courtroom my thoughts were all over the place. I was hearing things about a man whom I had once thought the world of. How could I have been so wrong about someone? Why aren't people made aware of the specific things to look for to stop child abuse happening? And why isn't more help offered? Questions kept running through my mind, but I could find no answers.

I believe that people need to be made aware of the things to look for. My advice would be to watch for someone who makes a child feel extra special, silly little games especially tickling games, and people need to be able to question why someone would take such an interest in their children. Parents and people who are working with children need to be made aware of the specific things of what to look for. If this happens then I believe that child abuse can be cut down significantly.

Michael Hawes

21/10/03

<u>Peter's account</u>: Peter is 17 at the time of writing this.

<u>Jeff Carney</u>

My first memory of Carney was in a school assembly when I first arrived at the school in reception. He introduced the new kids to the school, which on this occasion included Mike and I, and he called us 'little rabbits'. I turned round to him and said, 'I'm not a rabbit, you are!' as little kids do.

I first saw the 'close relationship' with the family when my older brother went to stay with Carney and go swimming after school with him. My 'relationship' with Carney developed when I was in junior school. He used to take us home after school some nights, but that would sometimes mean having to stay in school for a while longer. He often bought me sweets from the local shop on the way home as well. This continued to happen up to the point when my parents were getting divorced. We went on holidays with him to Padstow and Polzeath (Cornwall) and St David's in Wales. When the time came for all of us to move house, my dad stayed at home, my sister, brother and mum went to a friend's house while Mike and I went to stay with Carney. This went on for about six months. During this time we were still at his junior school (St Sebastian's), where he took us to and from school, occasionally meeting up with the other family members. Whilst staying with him, I never mentioned the fact that I was to friends at school, but we were staying with a 'special friend'. I was treated like a very special

116

person at his house, being 'spoilt' with sweets and 'affection'. We sometimes went to London on the train to see visitor-attraction centres, such as the Tower of London and the London Dungeon. We went to the Hexagon in Reading to see concerts as well. One Christmas, Mike and I were elves for Brian Stephens' nursery, with Carney being Santa Claus.

I didn't have any suspicions of Carney back when we knew him, as I always thought he was the caring head teacher, who later became a friend of the family. Looking back, it doesn't surprise me, as I was one of his 'special friends'. He also 'cared' about many children, notably ones with problems in their lives (e.g. parents getting divorced).

I now feel that, as Mike's twin brother, I was used as a shield, diverting focus from Carney's friendship with Michael. One thing I do remember is that he did give me money to spend on what I wanted, and stopped giving it to my mum, as his argument was she would spend it on clothes for me, which wasn't what I *wanted*. I knew of her basic financial situation, meaning that she didn't have much money being a single parent looking after four kids. This was also evident in that she went to work before I got up, and came back in time for dinner. That is why it didn't really bother me that she spent money for me on clothes, but Carney thought differently.

When the police arrived, at first I didn't know who they were or why they were here. When the officer said she was from the Child Protection Unit of Thames Valley, I felt shocked and instantly thought of three people: Carney, my dad and my friend Alastair – not in that particular order. It

117

had to be someone I knew well from where we used to live, and these were the only people I had kept in touch with. I knew it couldn't have been my dad or my friend, as they interviewed my mum, which left Carney. As the interview developed, she asked where I used to live, Carney's name came up, and she went straight down that road of questioning about him. At first, I was very shocked – which was helped by a few beers after the interview!

To be honest, I had forgotten about the day of the June court case, as quite a few months had passed and I was over the first bit of shock, but I was also concentrating on my exams. When I heard my mum on the phone talking about it, I instantly remembered. When she said no imprisonment for a sentence, I thought she was joking, but then it dawned on me that he had got away with what he had done. I felt let down by the justice system and betrayed by the trust I had of him. I wanted justice to be served. Having admitted to some of the charges, I was very surprised he didn't go down for what he did, and I could have killed him if I'd seen him.

I supported Mum's campaign from the beginning, as the effect on our family, the stress and tension it had caused was huge. That was just one family. Many others were involved. As soon as the case was referred to the Courts of Justice, I was always going to go without any doubt in my mind. On the day of the hearing, I was overawed by the fact that I was actually there, and then by the number of cases that had been referred, not to mention many other cases that hadn't because the sentences were just lenient, not unduly lenient.

During the hearing, I felt as if one of the judges knew who we were and why we were there. This was because he was facing the barristers and looking at me, just as I was facing the barrister and looking at him. I felt disgusted that any barrister could be defending the defendants for any of the cases, especially the one who was defending Carney, as I knew the effect it has had on me personally and on the family.

The media presence didn't really bother me, as it felt they were also supporting my mum as I was, but also doing their job. I was glad that people who didn't know the real Carney soon would, and make his life a living hell as he has done to so many others.

I hope for the judges to be as hard on Carney as possible, but would be happy for a prison sentence, as the high judges would have seen the injustice of this case.

Peter Hawes

21/10/03

And so over to Roger. It is interesting how people live together as families under one roof, and still we don't communicate our thoughts. Talking to each other is not the same as communicating. Communicating is about reaching each other. Listening is not the same as hearing. Listening requires thought – anyone can hear, if they have the sense of hearing!

Chris, being older, now aged 23, is getting on with his career, and has worked 'it' through, whatever his 'it' was.

Nicky, now aged 21, had her private hell in 2002 coming close to death. Now studying at Durham University, she feels relieved that justice has at last happened, although the sentence should have been far longer. She is pleased that all now know the truth, finally. Even as a 6-year-old, her uneasy and uncertain instincts about Jeff were correct and she would not be convinced otherwise by anyone. Yes, she was young, but she was right. We, as adults should have listened to her more intently, and questioned ourselves. Remember that, if you find yourself in a similar situation one day.

Roger's account:

Never Take NO for an Answer.

Marilyn has already explained my involvement in this affair yet I felt that perhaps it might be interesting to understand my thoughts as a new husband to Marilyn and stepfather to the boys and Nicky.

Even before I met Jeff I knew what he was from listening to Marilyn speaking about him. Conversations about Jeff took place at every meeting with friends and, without question, the women supported him and all the men asked questions and had doubts. Jeff was presented as a unique and unusual man looking for quality relationships without any sexual demands. He must be gay they would all tell me. My understanding of gay men, having a gay son, is that they are passionate, very touchy-feely and openly enjoy female company; it's just that their sexual juices are different from heterosexual men.

Marilyn is a vibrant and attractive woman who demands attention from whoever she communicates with. She is very passionate and warm with people. She likes to 'touch' just to check that the other person is with her, so to speak. In talking about Jeff, it became clear that he was not into touching Marilyn as a normal man would be, he was very clearly into touching the twins in a highly visible and playful manner. Nothing like a surrogate father or mature uncle; it was about children's fun and his role in that fun.

Before I finally made my commitment to Marilyn I took a three-month break because I just knew what he was and what I would have to deal with someday in the future. Could I cope?

Once Marilyn and I became engaged I met with Jeff and immediately he knew that I was uncomfortable with him and after the macho handshake he played with Michael in a way that I had never done with any of my children. I was very uncomfortable. I saw him lying on top of Michael without touching as if he was about to have intercourse. Hands down the back of Michael's trousers and touching in a way that was an indication of interest in his personal regions. All presented as a game. What a nice man! I felt uncomfortable, with a great desire to throw him out of the house. I knew if I did this at this time, Marilyn would have supported Carney, so I had to bide my time.

I explained to Marilyn my thoughts and we simply agreed to differ. One evening we went round to his house for tea and when we arrived he had Michael across his lap in his shorts with his hand down the back of the shorts. Carney knew I understood what he was and he was playing

121

a game of strength showing me that he had control. In a flash Peter, who was also in the room, looked across at me and it was like he had seen the light. Michael then got the message and moved away from Carney. Without a word being spoken, we had broken the spell. As we began to leave the house, Carney called Michael up to his room to give him a present. I heard him telling Michael how he loved him. Something snapped in me and I ran up the stairs, grabbed Michael and rushed him into the car. That was the end. Then we moved to Sussex and the matter was suspended until the police arrived.

Having survived the interrogation with the police, the changes in Marilyn began to take place. Firstly denial, then how it was all her fault, followed by 'what an awful mother I am, best thing I can do is to kill myself!' Some of this I saw, but the potential suicide I missed.

Then one day, following a meeting at the doctor's, I said to Marilyn that she was right – it was her fault! It was like a volcano erupting, but it lanced the boil, and from that moment on she moved into anger, which was the beginning of the healing process.

Great, I thought, get back to work and earn some money. No such luck, as the court hearing took place in April, followed by the Crown Court in July, with no custodial sentence! Marilyn was simply confused, angrier, disillusioned and felt totally let down. She became very difficult to talk to and quite reclusive at that time. Then one day she began to write letters, and once the first response came in she began to heal. The complete one-woman campaign began her healing process and it moved from anger towards Jeff into anger with the system. When that happened the campaign really gained strength, Marilyn became articulate, very logical and strong. From then on, I saw another woman, with passion and strength in everything she did. She now has a complete range of new skills on display – pity that it took a trauma to bring it all out! Not the woman I first met, who carried uncertainty and doubt, but a charismatic, charming and energetic woman. The one she was always meant to be!

As for the boys, the whole process was quite difficult. I decided I should manage the situation like a project. We had meetings run like mini business meetings to discuss the issues. How they felt, and how it would affect their mother. At sixteen going on seventeen, I treated them like men, and we had many serious and sensitive discussions.

As the time went on there would be days when Michael, especially, would be very emotional and tearful, so we would have another meeting. I did not give any opinions. I just made sure that they understood the situation and what was going to happen. Then we began to have a chat in the pub, with a few drinks easing the conversation. This is when I started to say, 'Spit it out, boys!' At first they were reticent, and then Peter began to talk, and the elder brother, Chris, made it clear that he understood the situation and it became a debate when it all came to the surface.

One Monday evening we were all in the pub and suddenly, without reason, Mike verbally attacked and abused his mother. This was the moment! Peter took Marilyn home whilst Chris and I stayed with Michael in the pub. Almost on the point of spitting it out – but not quite. Then we got the date for the Appeal Court hearing and Mike invited me for a drink and spat it all out. For him it was all about Jeff undermining his confidence in his mother, having already lost his dad in the divorce. Very wicked behaviour by Jeff designed to keep him in control.

We then decided to take the twins to the Appeal Court hearing, which was a great idea. Hearing seven cases and realising what it was all about gave them knowledge and understanding that other children had experienced worse abuse. Then Harriet Harman, the reporters, barristers et al., gave them so much support. It was rebuilding their confidence. They could now talk about what had happened in a positive way, and the experience would stay with them for life, as will the message. Whatever the odds, you can win through, regardless of the challenge if you have a mind to!

Through this whole experience, I would speak with Nicky and Chris every week to check the emotional temperature and agree this week's strategy. Whilst this may sound clinical, it was the way to put some structure and process to a very sensitive and emotional situation. I hope that we have all learnt how to handle a difficult situation should we ever be unfortunate enough to have another traumatic experience. We were a team – no, we are a family.

12

Looking Back and Moving On

As I write the final adjustments to this book, it is now New Year's Eve 2003. A time when, metaphorically, we all 'close the book and begin a new one'. *This* book is definitely being closed tonight! I welcome 2004 with a warm and open heart.

Looking back is not something I would normally recommend, but at times it is necessary in order to move on. I suppose you could say, reflect and reassess. There is little point in having regrets, because you can't rewrite history. Hindsight is a qualification we would all do well to have as a first-class honours degree. If I had known then what I know now, what would I have done differently?

The answer is – everything, because I am different now. Then, I was vulnerable for a variety of reasons. If my life was to take the same course again, I could not, and would not, change anything. When your life goes pear-shaped, it is difficult to have the same logic, and instincts become dulled. Your thoughts are distorted. You are a target for abuse because you are needy.

I will never know how it has, in real terms, affected my boys. Every success they have from here on will relieve my mind; every failure will cause me angst. Roger tells me Michael has found it hardest to accept the untruths Jeff was saying about me over the years, enabling him to groom Michael. How can anyone tell lies to a child about their parent? Implying I found him difficult, implying I didn't love him. It is absolutely wicked and evil. Whatever the manifestation of someone's sexual sickness, to work on a child's mind, placing a wedge between parent and child is disgraceful. However, why was I surprised? That is how grooming works. That is why it is so damaging. What an awful betrayal of friendship to have experienced at only 17.

Two months on, it still amazes me, shocks me, stuns me and freezes me to think how powerfully effective and destructive grooming is. It is a crime, which stands alone from any other. It is, without doubt a serious, abusive, manipulative offence. It comes with a deliberate and thought-through strategy.

What have I learnt? Never ignore your instincts – respond to them, respect them, listen to the inner voice and don't ignore it.

I have also learnt, no matter how angry and negative I felt at the time, that it is possible to put anger positively to good use. Righteous anger, as Father William would say.

I believe it is necessary to forgive in order for real healing to take place, in any situation. Of course, I can never forget what has happened; it is *how* you remember the issues which has importance. If you remember with anger, then you haven't forgiven, and it will eat away at your life like a cancer and cause all types of illnesses. 'Disease' means dis-ease, a lack of peace within. We must let go and move on in order to heal.

Jeff is no longer my problem. He must wrestle with his conscience and one day face his Maker, as we all must. I referred earlier to Matthew, Chapter 18, verses

3 to 12, and, as Father William reminded me, it's chilling stuff. I feel I have forgiven Carney – I hope I am right. I have lost the anger toward him, but the hurt remains.

Whatever I have or have not done in my life, whatever I have or have not been, successes or failures, my children remain constantly my greatest achievement. I am intensely proud of all four, and love them with all my heart. Ultimately, this man damaged my children, friends and family, and everything I held true in life.

As any parent knows, if your child is hurting, for whatever reason, then the pain is three times as bad for you. Therefore, I am not sure if I can or will ever forgive the things he said to Michael about me. I know he rejected Nicky. What had been Michael's thoughts about his mother over the last seven years? He surely could not have enjoyed everything I was offering to him as his mum. He couldn't see the best in me; Carney had confused his young mind. It is no wonder his behaviour was so difficult to understand at times.

There have been occasions when I thought, and felt, that he loathed me and then absolutely loved me. It was far beyond any normal mood-swing changes during puberty – it was extreme. Thankfully, he is working it all through, as they all are. He has had a traumatic year – they all have. My heart still aches when and if I think about it for more than a few minutes, and the tears effortlessly roll. However, the children have all been hugely successful in various ways, in spite of Carney. None of us will roll over and die! They are a credit to themselves, and should be rightly proud of their strength.

On reflection, the law actually let Jeff down. Had the judge made a more appropriate decision, Jeff would have been spared much publicity, and settled down to serving his time.

Whatever human rights campaigners say, victims and defendants have rights, but they must be balanced. I am certain that paedophiles contain a sickness within, which people cannot understand, nor do they wish to do so. Sadly, this 'illness' manifests itself destructively onto our nearest and dearest. Nature's desire is to protect one's young; nothing else matters, it is primeval and animalistic – logic and reasoning have no place in the debate. Some people call paedophiles 'animals'. Not true. When do you ever see animals molesting youngsters, or indecently assaulting them sexually.

I have struggled with whether or not the good times we had with Jeff were all about manipulation. Maybe, maybe not – who knows? I can't wrap it up and put it in a box. There were times we all enjoyed – there were children he would have healthily helped. That is what makes it so sad. He had a real talent, which he misused and abused. Nothing in my life has caused me so much heartache and pain – nothing!

For different reasons, many of us were living a hell, which, although different, overlapped one another's. When we experienced our own 'black days', we still had to support each other if another one of us was also having one – friends, family and ex-colleagues alike. It became exhausting, depressing and draining, in every way imaginable. The after-effects from this abuse are like ripples in a pond – far-reaching. Nevertheless, through the disgust, horror and pain normality has to continue – you can't stop living. That's what makes it more tiring. Relationships must still function, you still have to eat, shop, wash, iron, tidy up, try to smile and laugh again. Daily life continues. It won't go away. That in itself is exhausting, and it is the same when people are bereaved – it is such an effort to think.

I know I should not have had to spend my summer

fighting for something which should be in place already – a strong legal deterrent! We cannot call ourselves a Christian country until we actively protect family values and ensure support for the well-being of our children.

I also believe, as the Buddhists do, that whatever happens to you – no matter how bad – in the end is the best thing for you. A very liberating thought. Clouds have silver linings. Maybe I was meant to do this. I am now actively involved in the campaign Enough Abuse, calling for zero tolerance, and together with Jo I have started a consultancy called Enough Abuse, advising adults and children what to look for and where to go if suspicious.

I remain angry and frustrated at the law in this country and the judiciary. I implore the lawmakers to move swiftly toward zero tolerance for the good of all. For this crime, no consideration or trade-off should be given for pleading guilty – the full facts should be made available to the judges, enabling right and proper sentencing, which must become much tougher on the offender. Much more medical research should be sought to positively help the offender from reoffending, or even from offending in the first place.

I believe that we are only beginning to tackle this hideous blight, slowly peeling back the layers of the onion, becoming more shocked at what we discover. We have a duty as a nation to find a resolution.

Here are a few proven facts that I have learnt from talking to respected researchers: 35% of Internet child-porn viewers are already abusing – that is more than 1 in 3. 100% of people arrested through Operation Ore were white males. Over 95% of paedophiles are white males. Very few are women – we are not predatory in the same way men are. In other countries, the penalties are so severe it appears to reduce the crime significantly.

It appears mainly to be a white, Western world disease. Hence the need for zero tolerance.

A postcode lottery exists with sentencing – depending which circuit judge and in which area your case is heard. No consistency! Magistrates recommend one action, referring the case to Crown Court, where the judge may say something different. In many cases the defendant walks away with less punishment than they would have received from the magistrate!

Looking forward and moving on, I shall continue campaigning until the law changes, and I hope there is a groundswell of support to put pressure on judges and government. Specific and extensive training should be given to all those who have to hear child-abuse cases, in order to fully understand the damaging, irrevocable effects. It *will* need funding – but what price do you place on a child's life and future? If a child's life is harmed because of this act of abuse whilst it is still developing, what chance does it have of entering adulthood as a rounded and balanced person?

We all belong to a network of friends and family – one day the doorbell may ring and your life may be changed forever. You and the life you knew will never be the same again. There will be no choice – I mean *forever*!

Having learnt over the last few months what abuse of this kind *really* does to a family, I am committed to working with child-help organisations in the future. Bizarrely, for some inexplicable reason I believe I have been called to be in this place right now.

I am currently unable to enter a church to attend a conventional service, not because of lack of faith, or belief, but for a different reason. Carney represented himself as a devout churchman. You will remember – church is where I first met him, and now I see him in

130

my mind all the time, at the altar rail, giving a sermon, sharing the peace, taking communion, holding the chalice, praying. It is like driving past a place on a road where a loved one has been dramatically killed – it takes a long time before one is able to pass by without it invading your heart and mind. I have tried, but I lose my inner peace, it becomes a pointless, emotionally stressful exercise, and so I regularly visit Alton Abbey, where the peace is tangible.

I steer clear these days of anybody who says, 'Trust me, trust me' – I did trust, and look where it got me! Anyway, why does it need to be said? Perhaps, a potential problem is being warned in advance!

This episode in my life has made me focus on what is important – I mean relationships and how we work them. Our family has been through hell, and yet we are stronger for all that has happened to us – we know we work together as an effective team. Having an honours degree, and a well-paid job with status, will not make anyone a better spouse, child, brother, sister, friend, parent or neighbour.

Without the past year, I would not have met people who have touched my life so positively. I would rather not have written this book, and I thank you for reading it. However, if it helps others and saves another family from the horrors of this experience, then it was a worthwhile thing to do. My heart aches for other families finding themselves in a similar situation, and those who are currently, and as yet unknowingly, already involved in it.

My friends and family have been truly amazing. I have now finished with my counsellor. We said goodbye a few days ago – a bittersweet moment. We had laughed and cried together. I am still on tablets, but that is my next task – to be pill-free! Time to move on.

If your life has been affected by abuse, of any kind, I hope you find the courage to move on in strength, eventually finding an inner peace.

All that is left to say is, Everyone has the absolute right to say NO. Everyone has the absolute right to challenge NO and find another route. If it matters, truly matters, believe in your strength and that of God, and don't let people deter you.

Never take NO for an answer.

Acknowledgements

Heartfelt and meaningful thanks to all of you who have helped me write this book, establish the Enough Abuse campaign and consultancy, supported me and kept me sane: my long-suffering list of family and friends – you know who you are; my dog, Max, who gives me a hero's welcome whenever he sees me; last, but by no means least, my loving, protective and ever-patient husband Roger!

My sincere thanks to: Child Protection Officers at Thames Valley Police; Dr Rebecca Dunne, my GP; Father William, my friend and Prior of Alton Abbey; Sarah Pickford, my counsellor; The Book Guild, my publishers and supporters of Enough Abuse campaign; Press and TV/Radio media, both local and national, especially Jason Collie of *Reading Evening Post*; Francis Maude MP; John Redwood MP; The Rt Hon Lord Goldsmith QC, Attorney General; Rt Hon Harriet Harman QC, Solicitor General; Researchers into Child Abuse, factual and medical; KCD Media Design, designers of Enough Abuse logo and printing; Coolwave Ltd, who freely provided our web technology and support.

In addition, campaign supporters; Robin Bynoe, Charles Russell law firm, London; Richard Simmons, Hacker Young Accountants, Hove.

Contact: www.enoughabuse.co.uk

We will do all we can to help you. We understand.